RATION BOOKS AND RABBIT PIE

LINCOLNSHIRE FOLK REMEMBER THE WAR

Edited by Linda Crust

Published by

THE SOCIETY FOR LINCOLNSHIRE HISTORY AND ARCHAEOLOGY

2008

First published by the Society for Lincolnshire History and Archaeology 2008

ISBN 978 0 903582 31 5

British Library Cataloguing in Publication Data

A CIP catalogue record for this book is available from the British Library

Front cover photograph by Dennis Peall

Designed by Nigel Kingston

Printed in the UK by F W Cupit (Printers) Limited
Horncastle, Lincolnshire

CONTENTS

ACKNOWLEDGEMENTS

This book would not have come into being without the willing co-operation of the women and men whose memories are recorded here. Their details are given on pages 5-7. The importance of recording oral testimony is emphasised by the fact that, very sadly, several of the interviewees have died since the recordings were made. We are grateful to their families for allowing their voices to live on through this book and hope that it is an adequate tribute to all these wonderful Lincolnshire folk.

The production of this book has involved many other people too. We offer particular thanks to the following individuals who undertook the oral recordings from which the extracts used in this book are gleaned:

Pam Allpress, Linda Crust, Jean Gates, Mary Hey, Bill Leaper, Janet O'Reagan, Dorothy Quantrell, Ken Redmore, Maisie Seward and Cheryl Steele.

Some of the above also transcribed the interviews, but the rest of this time-consuming task was undertaken by Linda Crust and Brenda Webster.

Many hours of recordings were made, from which Linda, assisted by Brenda, selected the extracts used. All of the original material, and the transcripts, have been deposited in the Library of the Society for Lincolnshire History & Archaeology at Jews Court, Lincoln, where they can be consulted, by prior arrangement.

The historic photographs and other material illustrating the text have come from a number of sources. We gratefully acknowledge permission from the following to use this material:

From Museum of Lincolnshire Life, by courtesy of Lincolnshire County Council: figs 2, 5, 7, 13, 15, 16, 17, 30, 38, 39 & 40; from the Local Studies Collection, Lincoln Central Library, by courtesy of Lincolnshire County Council: figs 11 & 14; Lincolnshire Echo: figs 34 & 35; P. Green: fig. 4; Ken Redmore: figs 8, 9, 10, 25, 27, 29, 33 & 44; Stewart Squires: fig. 37; Maureen Sutton: figs 23, 24, 28, 32, 40 & 43; Brenda Webster: figs 1, 3, 6, 12, 18, 19, 21, 22, 31, 36, 41 & 42; Peter Wilson: figs 10, 26.

Linda Crust, Ken Redmore, Brenda Webster & Catherine Wilson
March 2008

A surviving pill-box at Theddlethorpe St Helen, one of the few tangible reminders of wartime in Lincolnshire outside the airbases

CONTRIBUTORS

(in order of first appearance in text)

Clarice Driffill P. 11, 54, 69,
Bracebridge Heath

Clarice was born in Bracebridge Heath in about 1920. At the outbreak of war she was working in the offices of Campion's Garage in the city but later she helped the war effort as a packer at Smith's Crisps factory. She married a soldier and after the war they ran a garage in Tuxford, Nottinghamshire. She retired to Waddington.

Evelyn Hodson P. 12,
Tattershall Thorpe, 2005

Evelyn, the seventh of eight daughters, was born at Leagate, Coningsby, on 17th August 1931 where she still lived during WWII. Despite the austere climate of the time she vividly remembers a very happy childhood, leading up to her first year of work during the last stages of the war.

Noreen Farrow
Alford, 2005 P. 14, 22, 46

Noreen was born in North Somercotes on 1st March 1930 and has lived in Alford for over 30 years. She has 4 daughters and 12 grandchildren. She spends much time with her family and also playing bowls and bridge.

George Smith P. 14, 24, 36, 58, 66,
Tattershall Thorpe, 2005

George was born on 12th September 1911 and came to the county as a young man in 1933. He lived at Tumby during WWII and worked as a driver of steam threshing sets, steam ploughs and steam rollers. His memories of this time make compulsive listening.

Kit Lawie P. 15, 16, 26, 59, 66,
Toynton All Saints, c1950

Kit (nee Shaw) was born at Brickyard Farm, East Keal, near Spilsby in 1928 and continued living there throughout the War. After her marriage in 1953 she moved to nearby Toynton All Saints, where she has lived ever since. She is a keen local historian.

Joyce Crisp P. 16, 28, 35, 63.
Stickford

Joyce (nee Baldock) was born on a farm in Stickford in the mid-1930s and was thus only a child at the time of the War. She has always lived in the Boston area and has retained strong ties with her home village.

Joan White   P 18 43.
Willoughby, 2005

Joan was born in 1917 and moved to Willoughby in 1935 to teach in the village school. She married into the White family, who own the garage and lawn mower services. She is a fine craftswoman and has been involved in the Parish Council and Women's Institute.

May Wise   P 18, 19, 20.
Stickney

May was born in 1912. She and her husband farmed their smallholding in Stickney throughout the War, moving to Langrick in 1952. She was probably best known in Stickney for working with her sister in the local fish and chip shop (Wright and Wise) for several years.

Ellen Jackson   P 21. 32,
Tattershall, c1940

Ellen was born in Holland Fen (south of the Witham) and lived in Coningsby during World War II. She particularly enjoyed cycling around her local area.

Spilsby Woman   P 34.

This lady spent much of the war working as a nurse at Lincoln County Hospital. Afterwards she returned to her home area near Spilsby and married.

Richard Sharpe   P 27, 48, 61.
Anwick

Richard was born at Anwick in 1927 where his father worked the Anwick Manor Farm. After training at Agricultural College, Richard eventually followed his father, farming the same land. He married Gill and their son is now a farmer in his own right in Lincolnshire.

Dorothy King   P 30, 36, 38, 50.
Spilsby, 2005

Dorothy, born in 1918 in Spilsby, was the daughter of John King, a local grocer, Methodist local preacher and magistrate. As a girl she attended Spilsby Grammar School. Dorothy grew up to be an independent single woman, proud of her business ability and with a great interest in local history. She now lives in a residential home with her beloved cat.

Hilary Healey   P 31, 45, 68.
Nocton, 1946

Hilary was born in Grantham on 14th January, 1935. The family moved to Nocton in 1943. Hilary attended Lincoln School of Art and later taught at Spalding Girls' High School until 1975, when she turned an interest in archaeology into a full-time job. She has an interest in medieval pottery and enjoys painting, drawing and writing.

Joan Parish P32.
Willoughby, 2005

Joan was born in Willoughby into the well-known Toyne family and was always part of the very fabric of village life. She supported many local groups and was deeply involved in the production of the Willoughby History Book.

Vera P34, 39, 65.
Halton Holegate

Vera enlisted with the WAAF and served mainly as a driver at a series of bases in Lincolnshire, including Scampton and East Kirkby. She lives in the Spilsby area.

Dot Hurdman P39, 54.
Willoughby, 2005

As a child Dot lived near the railway and later worked in the office at Willoughby Station. She married into a local farming family and has always taken an interest in village events especially the WI. Her hobbies are gardening and flower arranging.

Edith Taylor P40
Spilsby, 2005

Edith was born during the First World War and has lived almost all her life in Spilsby. During the Second World War she worked part-time in a local shop, but afterwards became a full-time housewife with plenty of outside interests, including the WI.

Ernie Bogg P46, 61,
Maltby le Marsh, 2006

Ernie was born in Farlesthorpe near Alford in November 1933. Educated at Alford, he left school at 14 to work for Fenton & Mould, caravan builders. He then worked for A Wood & Sons, builders, for 45 years. He lives in Maltby le Marsh with his second wife, Hazel.

Margaret Harrison P48, 68.
Willoughby, 2006

Margaret was born in Willoughby in 1935 into the old-established Freshney family. At 18 she left for nurse training in Manchester and after marriage moved to North Hykeham where she was involved in organising the Community Volunteers and was on the District Council. She later trained as a Methodist Minister. On retirement she returned to the village and was instrumental in forming the History Group.

Bob Riddington P53.
Willoughby, 2005

Bob was born in Willoughby in 1925 to a musical family. He has lived in the village all his life and was the local milkman. He is a gifted natural musician playing at Alford Methodist Church and many other venues. He is well-known locally for his wit and humour.

Clarice Rutter P 54, 67,
Whaplode, 2005

Clarice was born 17th January 1933. She spent her early life, and the war years, at Cranesgate Farm, Whaplode. She attended Holbeach C of E Girls' School, but left school at the age of 14 to work on the family farm. In 1953 she moved with the family to Manor Farm, Maltby le Marsh. She remained actively involved in farming, becoming a judge for cattle, poultry and goats. She continues to live in Maltby le Marsh.

Dolly Wheatley P 55, 56,
Lincoln, 1948

Dolly was born in the London suburb of South Norwood in 1908 and moved to Lincoln at an early age. During the War, despite the task of running the family home - she had three school-aged children - she worked at Clayton DeWandres and took on a succession of part-time jobs, including ARP work. In the 1950s she and her husband moved to their small-holding at North Greetwell.

Henry Wheatley P 55, 57,
Lincoln

Henry, son of Dolly, was born in Spa Street off Monks Road, Lincoln, in 1928 and has always lived in or close to the city. During World War II he attended the City School and later served an apprenticeship at Ruston & Hornsby. His working career included spells with Rustons, the police force and British Waterways.

FOREWORD

It gave me great pleasure to be asked to write this foreword for a Society publication based on work carried out by a team of its members. It is especially pleasing to note that the idea originated from members of the Society's Local History team, who later organised two day workshops, with tuition provided by the East Midlands Oral History Archive. One of the objectives the Society has set itself is to foster Lincolnshire local history groups, and the workshop was attended by members of several of these groups, some of whom subsequently took part in the project. It was agreed that the topic of the second world war would attract a lot of interest among those willing to record their youthful recollections, as well as among many readers. Since servicemen and women have already recorded and written copiously on this topic, the project focused on civilian life, and this has also redressed the balance in favour of women's wartime experiences.

Lincolnshire County Council funded the purchase of minidisk recorders, which were lent out by the Society to several of the groups and also used by individuals elsewhere. Recordings were made of about two dozen people. Transcripts were in some cases made by interviewers, but the bulk of the transcription was carried out by Linda Crust, who also selected the extracts and added the commentaries on them. We are deeply in her debt and very lucky to have had the benefit of her considerable experience of this kind of work. Brenda Webster, Ken Redmore and our indefatigable President, Catherine Wilson, also gave considerably of their time and knowledge, including in relation to illustrative material.

Older readers will be taken back to their youth. As George Smith says near the end of the book, 'You forget you know'. For those who were young adults during the war, the worry, the heartache and the shortages will come back, but also the sense of comradeship and optimism and the making of new friendships.

For those who were children, perhaps the excitement of those times will predominate, since, on the whole, children in Lincolnshire were lucky enough not experience much fear. The anonymous speaker who lived in Anwick Fen reminded me of old telegraph poles and the like strung out across my grandfather's longest field as a precaution against enemy landings. The man in Farlesthorpe, who stayed above ground because he had been buried in a trench during the First World War, brought back the way in which, during night-time alerts, my father would see my mother and myself safely into his glasshouse stoke hole, and then go off and walk among half an acre of glass. One contributor was a nurse at Lincoln County Hospital when the Nurses' Home received a direct hit. I remember hearing what we thought was that bomb, whistling as it went down from an aircraft directly overhead. It was said that bombs you heard were going to fall elsewhere, but I took no chances and, unbidden, got behind my grandmother's settee so I would not get caught in any flying glass.

I am not at all sure what my children and grandchildren will find most interesting in this book. Perhaps they will feel that they have met the owners of these voices, for one is left in no doubt that the print represents spoken words. The hesitations, the simple descriptions, the changes of tone as something else is suddenly remembered, even the overlapping of similar experiences must evoke a deeper understanding of what the war was like for civilians in Lincolnshire, how it enveloped absolutely everyone in some way or other, and often quite deeply. If we exclude terrorist activities, the only 'war' that the younger generations experience is from overseas through the TV screen in the sitting room.

In Ration Books and Rabbit Pie, I am sure it will seem more realistic, more immediate, more personal, and better visualised. I wish the contributors and the team every commercial success the book deserves.

Dennis Mills
Branston, February 2008

INTRODUCTION

World War II officially began on 3rd September 1939, but throughout the 1930s events had been leading up to it. The outbreak of war with Germany was announced over the wireless at 11 o'clock that Sunday morning. It did not come as a surprise to the people of England.

Government plans were already afoot to prepare civilians for the unknown future. The Home Front was to be motivated and defended. The Government tried to prepare the civilian population to deal with a strange and frightening future by posting leaflets containing information and instruction through every letterbox. Posters and the wireless played a large part in disseminating news and boosting morale. The civilian population experienced unprecedented government control over their diet, shopping, building work and even conversation ('Careless talk costs lives'). How did these things affect the people of Lincolnshire?

Families were sometimes separated as young men and women were called up for National Service. Unfamiliar sights, sounds and emotions were experienced. There was not a soul who had no knowledge of the conflict – nobody could be unaffected. Yet the people of Lincolnshire took their defence of the Home Front in their stride. True, as a rural county, food rationing seemed to cause little grumbling. There were gardens and rabbits and local food so, although the country's island status meant that our reliance on imported food had to be lessened, in this part of the country it was hard to find anyone who remembered any actual suffering through poor nutrition. In any case our population at that date was reared to be hardy and economical.

The evidence of war was never far away with the county full of aerodromes and servicemen. Land was requisitioned and electricity was first brought to some villages because of adjacent searchlight camps; American soldiers and airmen brought chewing gum and some glamour to village dances. Everyone from a child collecting salvage to an old man fire-watching was united in being pro-British and anti-Hitler. In this sense we all had something in common. We all wanted to protect the Home Front.

This book is the record by some people of Lincolnshire remembering their lives in a world war. Everyone had some individual experience of how things were. There are thousands more lives unrecorded but this is a sample of what happened here, in Lincolnshire, between 1939 and 1945.

Ellen Jackson of Tattershall in her Land Army uniform, 1940

CHAPTER 1

WAR BEGINS

Gas masks; men returning from Dunkirk; near loss of a family member; evacuees

The Prime Minister, the Rt. Hon Neville Chamberlain announced, by wireless, that England was at war with Germany on 3rd September 1939. Except for the the reserved occupations, all men in Britain aged 18-41 immediately could be called up, though in practice it was the youngest first. The previous July a trial black-out run had been ordered across the country.

Clarice Driffill

I married during the war – 30th December, 1939. But the anxiety of the war was for me, as a young person, and I think most young people of my age then, was 1938 when we didn't know whether there was going to be a war. You know, when Chamberlain went to Munich and come back and I can remember the tension of that year and we had practised blackout in town and you know we had to collect a gas mask and things like that. They were preparing and I think everybody – well there was a quietness and I remember Frank saying to me 'We'll go to the pictures one night' and we went in town and it was blackout. It was practice blackout, it was the summer of 1938, and we went to the pictures and, walking through the town, you would have thought the war had started because it was – everybody was waiting and didn't know.

And then I remember Chamberlain coming home and waving the paper as it's always talked about and him saying that there wasn't going to be a war and it was as if a bubble had burst and everyone started being noisy

"I'm - digging me garden and making twice as many vegetable patches"

Fig 1
The cover of a booklet issued by the Ministry of Agriculture as part of the 'Dig for Victory' campaign. This was a simple guide aimed at helping every family, regardless of the size of their gardens, to grow their own vegetables.

and the world had sort of come back to life and I think myself, and I think a lot of the young men in the village, boys (as were young men), I think they'd all been so tense because we'd none of sort of …that age, when you're young you can't visualise.

I know my parents did and I can remember my father saying 'There'll be this and that and the other,' and we couldn't believe it. You couldn't visualise. And that's right I can remember the happiness and yes, everybody laughing, 'Oh, it's all over. We're not going to have a war' – that attitude. And it was a lovely summer that year. It was towards the end of the summer; everybody seemed real happy again and – but I can always remember my father saying, 'Huh – it's not over yet.' He said 'You can forget him' he said. 'It's going to come – that bit of paper's nothing' he sort of said. He says 'Well I'm preparing for it. I'm – digging me garden and making twice as many vegetable patches.'

In 1941 the majority of adult women under the age of forty were called up for war work which was extremely diverse. This included married women but excluded those with young children. In 1943 the age of eligible women was extended to fifty.

They said go now down to Smith's Crisps and there's work there because they was sending loads and loads of crisps to France for the soldiers. Smith's in Bracebridge. And they said 'Stay there until we contact you' they said 'and we're preparing somewhere at Grantham for munition work and you'll be transferred there.'

Then they provide buses for you to go on munition work to Grantham unless you do other war work. So I went to Smith's Crisps like and worked there and we'd to be there at eight in the morning and I was never finished till eight at night. We was twelve hours. I was labelling the tins and getting them packed ready for the lorries. And we had to fill so many lorries a day for them to take down to the docks (I never knew where they took them). But we understood that's where they were going – to France.

"We all went together and were issued with our gas masks"

Fig 2
The interior of Smith's Crisp factory, Newark Road, Lincoln in the early 1950s. During the War, with large numbers of men absent serving in the armed services, local women were needed to keep essential Lincoln factories running.

Evelyn Hodson

I was born on 17th August 1931. I was one of eight girls called Manning. We lived in a Council house at Leagate Corner all through the war. My first recollection of anything to do with the war was our next door neighbour had some lodgers and they came to help build RAF Coningsby. This was before war was declared and they used to meet on Sunday nights and every time – 'Oh, if there's a war, it'll not last very long.' Same old story: 'It won't last longer than Christmas.'

The next thing was we had to be taken down to the school to collect a gas mask and this was the school where I attended in Coningsby. I remember distinctly seeing these piles of cardboard boxes with these gas masks in. My Mum, one or two of my sisters and the neighbours, we all went together and were issued with our gas masks which we were then responsible for and although I can remember collecting them, I cannot ever remember doing anything else with them other than buying special cases to put them in because as you got older they were more decorative than a cardboard box - but we did have to take them to school with us.

The next thing was the actual declaration of war. This I remember distinctly being a Sunday morning when we were in Chapel – we attended the Baptist Chapel service and Sunday School. One of my older sisters came along on her cycle (I was eight years old) and said that war had been declared. Of course I am easily panicked and I thought 'What does this mean?' To me, any minute, there would be people popping out of hedges and aeroplanes flying over but of course it never happened. We went home and had ordinary Sunday lunch and just sort of speculation of what would be expected of us but it all seemed to fizzle out because at that time we didn't have any boys in the family. I was the seventh of eight girls and most of the girls were out in service. They used to come home of a Sunday and so they would come home as usual for tea.

The next thing I remember is at school, the air raid shelters being built. They were long buildings put up in the playground. It was mixed. We had long, long shelters. I always make people laugh about this because this is

Fig 3
Alf Curtis, Frances Curtis and Geoff Barrett of Heighington trying out their gas masks. Children were expected to carry their masks at all times (note the carrying cases on the ground). Frances is wearing a 'Mickey Mouse' gas mask, specially designed for younger children.

where we had our first biology lesson because the Headmaster and a teacher used to meet in the air raid shelter. I was a bit naïve and didn't realise that this sort of thing went on. Mum and Dad had been quite happily married and I didn't realise that people did carry on with other people. So no name – but that was what happened and of course it became a laughing stock every time someone would see them go out.

The next thing was we started to get lots and lots of soldiers in the village and this would obviously be in 1940 because now I know it was they came back from Dunkirk and a lot of these that came back were from Wales and Shropshire. They were the KSLI – the King's Shropshire Light Infantry and absolutely full in the village. That was the first experience of lots and lots of men around. And obviously my elder sisters were of the age that went out with young lads and it caused a lot of consternation because the soldiers were much more exciting than the ordinary village boys. At this time there were still quite a lot of men in the village because they hadn't been called up – but they were starting to disappear.

I don't seem to remember too much about this time about the airforce. I do remember the first aeroplane that I saw. It was a Tiger Moth that I saw landing on the grass at RAF Coningsby and then, first of all during the war, a Hampden and, with hindsight you can say, it wasn't all that noisy – but to someone who'd had the quiet of the village – suddenly the air seemed full of funny noises which was of course the aeroplanes flying over.

It didn't worry us too much but they made the villages much busier and this of course is when the village started to change its shape because this corner had to be knocked down for the lorries to get round the corner, this house had to be knocked down because something ran into something else and

"Suddenly the air seemed full of funny noises"

Fig 4
A Tiger Moth biplane at Burnaston,
27 November 1945. This famous plane,
first manufactured by de Havilland in 1931,
was adapted for a variety of non-combative
purposes during the war and afterwards.

gradually it did change. We didn't suffer a lot of bomb damage. It was more damage from our own side because of changing the village to accommodate not only the RAF but all the soldiers in the village.

Noreen Farrow

Even as an eight year old in 1938 I realised there was going to be a Second World War. I remember Neville Chamberlain going to Germany to see Hitler in an attempt to avoid war. I remember the phrase 'Peace in our times' and people didn't believe it. My father thought of it as a breathing space and a chance to re-arm.

I also remember in 1937 or '38 a Zeppelin going up the east coast and seeing it from the window of my village primary school. In 1939 as a nine year-old I remember a lovely warm September morning playing in the garden. Then at 11 o'clock we went into the house and over the wireless Neville Chamberlain's immortal words 'We are now at war with Germany.' The rest of the day my father and his neighbour were busy making blackout shutters for the important windows in the houses.

"My father and his neighbour were busy making blackout shutters"

Certain occupations were immune from call-up and, because of the agricultural importance of the county, many men of call-up age were required to do service on the Home Front rather than in the armed forces.

George Smith

During the war I was working with steam engine, thrashing engine, engine driver all through the war and before the war actually.

When the war began I had to cycle to work in the dark when you couldn't 'ave a light. That were one of the worst things. And it meant you starting earlier in the morning because you see, those days you'd probably be ten, fifteen miles from home you see with a machine. Well, you'd got to cycle it and you'd got to be there, all ready, for seven o' clock, all ready. You see you'd got to tend engine for an hour before it was able to work properly. That's what made it much worse. They were not short of labour on the land before the war. The farmer that I worked for, men was accepted only during the thrashing season like, in the summer time you didn't get that. You had to find a job soft times. Sometimes I formed a gang and then gone sheep clipping or things like that. During the war we always had to go back to the shop for repairing machines, both our own and local farmers – repairing machinery. I did a bit of road rolling when they 'ad bombed places.

The Government ran a successful campaign to collect scrap metal, including saucepans. Patriotic housewives donated tons of utensils and railings were taken up all over Britain for the Spitfire Fund. Schools were generally allowed to retain metal railings if they enclosed a playground and railings and gates of village houses were spared if they were on the route of a milking herd of cows which might go astray and trample precious vegetable gardens if no fence restricted them.

As Kit remarked, most of this metal was ultimately dumped in the North Sea as it was unsuitable for recycling but, at the time, people felt they were making a personal contribution to building aeroplanes.

Kit Lawie

Well, I suppose in 1936, I'd be eight then, and we lived at Brickyard House up the Old Bolingbroke road and farmed up there – and farmed the hill of Marden which overlooked East Keal – to the north of Keal. And it was the high point really that we could see the coastline and across the fens. But the particular day that I remember in 1936 was really – I remember the date only because it was the day my grandfather died but it was also the date that the Graf Zeppelin went over and that was June 26th, 1936. The people in the village, the older ones that remembered the First War shook their heads and said that this is really a bad sign. The Germans are re-arming again and they're coming over here spying and so on. And of course it built in me something of the coming of the stress of the war I suppose and by 1939, when I was eleven, we were into war of course and I stood at Granny's gate down at the Carrs on the main road and watched a little local lorry – I'm not sure if it wasn't George Cheetham the coal and corn merchant – collecting the Territorials from East and West Keal. And they were all jolly lads waving to us but Granny, remembering the First War of course, was very sad to see them go and she'd plucked them some lads' love and given them as a good luck sprig each. We reached up to this lorry I remember. But they went off very happily. I suppose these boys hadn't been further than ten miles from home in their lives – most of them. They'd worked in the village – some of them had worked on the land with us. So off they went and Granny said 'Oh, it'll be all over by Christmas.'

"Oh, it'll be all over by Christmas"

Fig 5
Threshing by steam traction engine at Rutter's Farm, Huttoft, 1937, with Norman Hundleby on the engine. This was a very common sight in the Lincolnshire countryside throughout the autumn and winter months.

But then she said 'We said that last time, the beginning of the First War' and, talking to an eleven year-old child, I saw that she was very upset. But we had no electricity at the Brickyard where I lived, nor did she down on the main road, or no telephone. All we depended on was this quaint old radio that well, I think we called it a wireless in those days. It had two sections to it and it was on this … accumulators that we had charged then.

Within a day or two the scrap iron lorry came round collecting all the stuff, presumably for munitions. We thought they were going to be made into big guns I suppose, and the implements from the yard that were no longer any use, they collected them. I suppose, in retrospect – knowing they were never used and dumped in the North Sea – after the war we would have been a bit more cynical. But no – we gathered everything there was.

"I remember all the signposts had been taken away"

And the next thing I remember in all the lanes and the corners were the signposts being taken down, especially I was sorry to see a pretty little finger signpost, the old-fashioned ones, being taken away and I said to Mother 'If I'd known I'd have gone and taken it and brought it home and hid it until after the war.'

Of course the notices of 'Careless Talk Costs Lives' were plastered up everywhere and we children at school were really abuzz with the possibility of spies among us. We thought everybody that was a stranger, especially if they had a long mac or a trilby – we thought he'd got to be a spy if he asked the way somewhere and we didn't tell them. We were told we mustn't direct them anywhere. Or we told them completely the wrong direction if we thought we'd tell them something.

Between May 27th and June 4th, 1941, as the Germans closed in on them, over 335,000 British soldiers were evacuated from the beaches of Dunkirk in France to England in a variety of marine crafts large and small. This was known as 'the miracle of Dunkirk'. Men landed on beaches on the south and east coast and, from their landing points, parties of men walked or rode through the country dropping soldiers off near to their homes for leave and a short period of recovery. Village halls and schools were made available en route for impromptu camps to house the weary men. During this week of retreat, on June 10th Italy joined Germany and declared war on Great Britain and France.

Kit Lawie

One day at school I remember most particularly during the war. I was at West Keal school and, from the Boston direction there marched a company of soldiers of the Argyll and Sutherland Highlanders.

I remember the man in charge of them, Captain James O'Hearnson and I remember he walked in front ... and said, 'I commandeer your school. Will you all go into one room.' I thought – well this is going to be something – and he was in a kilt – he was in dress uniform which amazed me but it turned out that they'd been brought over from Dunkirk. They hadn't been landed lower down in Essex, they'd been landed at Kings Lynn by some boat that had set out presumably. And they'd marched for three days from Kings Lynn stopping somewhere at night I suppose and this was the third stop I gathered, West Keal school, and so they came and we were absolutely agog with sixty soldiers. I'd be about twelve, thirteen at the time – no I wouldn't be that – but anyway – I was impressionable shall I say among a bunch of soldiers.

The next morning they were still there; they'd slept in the playground. I suppose the officer and the batman probably had the infant room and they'd set up this cookhouse which we all eyed as they were hotting their beans up in their tin cans. And he came and spoke to us again – very imperial it was…and said 'Now what service can I do before I leave you all?' And the head teacher said 'Well, you could dig us a dugout if you like, to get in during air raids.' And these sixty men, in about half an hour, dug a complete dugout – a zigzag dugout in the playground. Then we went to the gate and said farewell to them. And they were marching to Hull – well, eventually, they'd be having another stop. And they were going to go on to Hull docks from invasion.

Joyce Crisp, who was a child at the time, mis-remembered the speaker of the announcement (Neville Chamberlain). Mr Winston Churchill (as he then was) became Prime Minister (not President) and Minister for War in 1940.

Joyce Crisp

When the war broke out me Mum was stood in the house. She was doing some baking for us because we had to do all our own cooking and baking. You didn't buy nothing because you couldn't get out. She was doing some cooking and we had the wireless on. That was all we'd got in those days. And there was, I think it was the eleven o'clock news, it was President Churchill whatdyacallhim, Churchill anyway, he came on and said he'd an announcement and war had broke out. It was eleven o'clock. I can't remember what day in particular. I remember that we was all stood round the table because we were supposed to be helping me Mum bake and getting in the way. The news caused her to have, oh I'll not say sour face, but just a

straight face. That was – because we'd been aware of it coming, like what with getting the drome built and getting the blockhouse built – that and the blockades up the road. They were all getting ready for it so we knew about it.

Nothing changed on the farm when war broke out. No, not really – not for the worse anyway. It changed for the better if anything because everybody had to take in what lodgers they could for to work at the aerodrome for to get it built. And then they had to take in what airmen they could, the ground force airmen. Some of the fliers came down with them. They brought their families with us like, they used to lodge - let their families have holidays with them, or whathaveyou. They used to have so long - so they was able to have their families down with us.

"These sixty men dug a complete zigzag dugout in the playground in about half an hour"

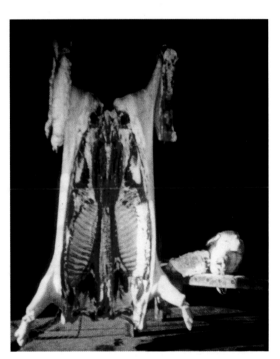

Fig 6
A pig carcass hanging on two steel hooks soon after the killing. To the right are the cratch (supporting wooden frame) and the pig's head. Pigs, which could be fed successfully off kitchen scraps and left-overs, were kept by a large percentage of country dwellers.

Of course they all got fairly good food with us making butter and, whathaveyou - you know, killing pigs and that. So it was fairly good living, considering, but it was short because you had to sell as much as possible because you needed the money. Because you couldn't go out - you couldn't earn nothing by going out to work. So you had to earn all your own money so you couldn't afford to eat it away, give it away.

"They were sure the Germans would be here before night-time"

Joan White

I was born in Manchester on the 7th of October, 1917 and from there I moved to Chesterfield and then to Grimsby and eventually to Willoughby, in 1935. I came here as a teacher at the village school and I have five children now, having married the village blacksmith in 1940 and I remember the beginning of the war – the day war broke out.

My husband and I had arranged to go to Grimsby, my home, to see my parents and

Fig 7
A gang of land girls taking a break from potato picking at Grange Farm (Flintham's Farm), Metheringham Heath. Potatoes were lifted from the row and spun clear of soil before being picked up by hand into baskets. The contribution of women on Lincolnshire farms, though resisted or even derided in some quarters, was very significant.

family. And of course it was announced that we were at war. His family were very much against us going to Grimsby then. They were sure the Germans would be here before night-time and it wasn't safe to travel. But anyway, he cut out some cardboard discs, with a slit in. And the slit lifted up and made a little hood over the hole; put them in front of the headlamps and that was the blackout that we had to use to travel in the dark. Not a very good light at all.

May Wise

When the war came on, well, we married in 1936 and the war broke out in 1939 didn't it? Yes, well, when the war broke out, the beginning of the war, my sister and her husband and me and my husband we was just thinking about starting a fish and chip shop then at Stickney, which we did. But as time went on, after two or three years, we got on very nicely for a start but after two or three years we couldn't get any supply of fish so we had to pack that in you see. But having said that, my husband he volunteered for the army but they wouldn't have him because he was in a reserved occupation. You see he was on the land, and so, and then, therefore, I had to work on the land as well because I had no family and so you was classed as single. You see you had to work on the land as well and that's what we were doing then. Well, we were potato picking and setting, and singling beet and everything you know, all the hand work. It was all hand work those days you see. All hand work, yes.

Well, we were quite lucky with rationing really because having him [husband] – he worked for a small farmer and they kept their own cows so of course we got a pound of butter each week you see. And we also, we was in a house at Stickney like and we had a pig sty. We kept our own pig. So for meat and butter and that sort of thing we didn't suffer at all really.

We slaughtered our own pig. Mind you, you had to get a licence. You had to have a licence to slaughter it you see. You had a man come to kill it but you had to have a licence you see and therefore you lost your tokens, what you would have had for meat like – you lost them.

But, as I say, we were quite lucky really to what some people were. We didn't suffer like they did in the towns. And we also had a big garden so we was able to grow a lot of vegetables.

There was the grocer's shop. There was just the chapel in between us and the grocer's shop so – handy for that. And I was quite friendly with the people that kept the shop. So that made a bit of difference you know. So, you know, we got on … We did not suffer really – not through rationing.

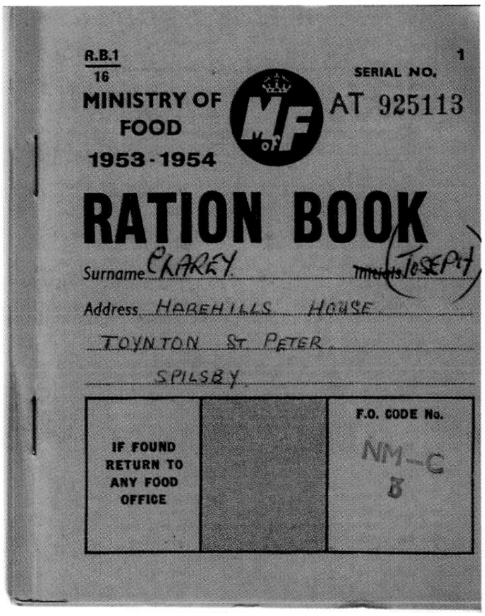

Fig 8
Scarce commodities, such as butter, milk, tea, sugar and cheese, were strictly rationed throughout the War. Rationing of all these items and, in addition, bread continued into the 1950s.

My eldest brother, no my second eldest brother. He was called up – as soon as he was eighteen he was called up – and he spent some time in Ireland. Because I shall always remember he was due to come home on leave, and the ship that he was due to come home in, it was sunk. Oh and my mother, she was, she thought he was on it and the next day, we lived near the railway line at Stickney, and the next day a train came in and I was playing near the railway line and I saw my brother – you know, he was waving out the window because he … The ship was too full and he couldn't get on that one and he was – yes, it was lucky wasn't it. Yes, he did. He got on the next one and he got home safely. Or else we thought we'd lost him.

Yes, that's, that was as near as any of us got – he was the only one really that was in the army. Because I suppose most of us on the land and it was a reserved occupation wasn't it you see?

I can remember, we had, where we lived, we had a lean-to glasshouse and it had a vine in it – lovely black grapes they were and, in the summer, well when they were ready my husband used to get them ready on a Monday night. And on a Tuesday night I used to – I had to go out to work, potato picking all day, come home and get washed and changed and get on my bike and take these grapes up to Boston to sell. For Leland's – it was Leland's in Red Lion Street at Boston where we used to take these. And, to us, it was a little fortune 'cos you see you couldn't import them – and they were lovely grapes. So we had quite an extra – it was quite an extra income really.

What we used to do we'd go brambling a lot. I used to make a lot of bramble jelly. But there again, you had to save up your coupons to get the sugar. That was the trouble. You know to get the – to make the jelly. That was just a few of things I remember.

"We slaughtered our own pig, but you had to have a licence"

On the subject of evacuees.

May Wise

As I say, we were a quiet village and we didn't … I think there were odd refugee children were brought into the village, but very few. You know you didn't get a lot of influx of any sort really. Not until we got the Dunkirk people. That was the biggest thing that happened as I remember. They were with us quite a few months, quite a few months. And of course they'd been away from their wives a long while you see. And the one that we had wanted his wife to come and stop – which she did. She came down and stopped quite a while like because … He was from South Shields. Yes, they was altogether different.

"Yes, they was altogether different"

This recipe was named after Lord Woolton, head of the Ministry of Food.

Woolton Pie

Ingredients:
1lb diced potatoes
1lb cauliflower
1lb diced carrots
1lb diced swede
3 spring onions
1 teaspoon vegetable extract
1 tablespoon oatmeal
A little chopped parsley

Method:
Cook everything together with just enough water to cover, stirring often to prevent it sticking to the pan. Let the mixture cool. Spoon into pie dish, sprinkle with chopped parsley. Cover with a crust of potatoes or wholemeal pastry. Bake in a moderate oven until golden brown. Serve hot with gravy.

From website:
'Frugal recipes from wartime Britain'

*'Those who have the will to win
Cook potatoes in their skin
Knowing that the sight of peelings
Deeply hurts Lord Woolton's feelings'*

CHAPTER 2

WAR ON THE DOORSTEP

Airfields; bombing; decoy aerodrome; POWs

Ellen Jackson

Yes, there was an airfield at Coningsby. Pete Phillip built one about two year after the war started because it was Stennetts' farm. It was Stennetts' farm, all grassland but they made landings on the grass for them for a start, and that sort of thing, you know. But I remember one night, coming home, one night we'd been on the … and it was moonlight and we did see – we knew he was there, we knew Jerry was about and our mud and stud cottage had a kind of piece of zinc over the top of it to keep the birds out. And we was, Mum was about – she was with me that night – we stood outside because we'd been stood outside and we was told to get in and the machine gun pellets from the Jerry rattled on the roof – that was a bit scary I can tell you. That was the worst experience we had I think.

We used to count the bombers going out and coming back in again, you know. I mean that one – I said that one came in that morning, it was late in, most of the others had been on ops and got in and this one, whatever she was – whatshallIsay M for Mother – and she was coughing very badly. ~~It was the Dakota~~ - *see* ~~she was coughing very badly~~ you know *above* spluttering and going...and you knew that sommut was wrong. Oh dear, I thought, something's going wrong –'Get over there boy, get over there. Don't come over here.' Because where we was it was grassland but … as much as anything you know ... it was terrifying. As Pete said it was very sad but it crashed.

It didn't get to the landing. It didn't get to the common. In fact they said that the rear ✱ gunner was dead before it left wherever it had been like. He'd been shot up. You got to know about these things because actually we used to go, we shouldn't have been, but girls in the Land Army was entitled to go on the camp and you could take friends with you. And I used to take another girl with me. If there was anything extra special we'd perhaps go for a couple of hours and that sort of thing.

✱ Dakota's were not armed

Spilsby Woman

In 1939-40 certain decoy aerodromes were established with the object of detracting attention from nearby operational dromes. Hagnaby was the decoy for Coningsby. There was approximately 30 personnel on the Hagnaby site – about a quarter of a mile from The Priory. The house was open house to anyone who wished to visit in an evening – and most evenings saw eight or ten lads coming to enjoy a log fire and comfortable surroundings. Mother always managed to provide some refreshment.

The decoy did receive some attention – particularly on the night when my brother was paying his last visit to his parents at home before going overseas.

"The machine gun pellets rattled on the roof"

The Anderson Shelter was a Government production named after Sir John Anderson, Home Secretary and Minister of Home Security in 1939. For those who could not afford the cost of them, they were provided free. A hole had first to be dug in the garden and the prefabricated corrugated steel structure was then erected. It was a cold, damp shelter for up to six people.

Noreen Farrow

"I heard the loudest bang of the War"

When we lived in North Somercotes we had an Anderson shelter in the garden. It was very often damp as we lived so near to the sea. It was at North Somercotes that I heard the loudest bang of the war. It was very frightening. Afterwards they said it was a landmine.

Towards the end of 1940 we moved to Sutton on Sea. It was a very sad year. Somehow we got most of our troops home from Dunkirk. France fell, Mr Churchill came to power and gave some inspiring speeches. I firmly believe, without Churchill, we would have surrendered. Lincolnshire became one large airfield and the country was very grateful. After the war we were the 'pancake county' – flat and boring. How short are memories.

On 29th September 1939 Russia and Germany had signed a Nazi-Soviet pact in Moscow approving the partition of Poland. ✱ On ~~October 6th~~ Germany invaded Moscow and the Russians then became our allies against Germany although they did not declare war against Japan until 8th August 1945 – three weeks before the allies declared victory over Japan. ✱ *June 1941*

Fig 9
An Anderson Shelter re-erected at the Museum of Lincolnshire Life, 2007.
The shelter was easy to erect and gave some protection from bomb blast and falling masonry.
It was always set below ground level in the garden and usually covered in soil
to increase its effectiveness.

Fig 10
A concrete pill box at Gibraltar Point, 2007.
Scores of boxes were placed at strategic points
along the Lincolnshire coast (some in fact survive
from the First World War). They were designed to
provide shelter for gunners of the mobile reserve
in the event of a successful landing by the enemy
on the coast.

The soldiers were billeted along the coast.
Pill-boxes with gun turrets were built on
pullovers [a pullover is an access route over
sand dunes or sea bank to the shore]. Soldiers
challenged you sometimes when you walked
home along the coast road home after going
to the pictures. We were not allowed to go to
the beach, I can't remember whether it was
just months or years that we couldn't see the
coast. We expected invasion and worried
what would happen if it happened.

Then in 1941 Hitler decided to invade Russia.
It was a great relief and I for one will always
be grateful for the fight the Russians put up – steel
the horrors they went through.

As a schoolgirl we had to get on with our
lessons and try and forget the awful news that
we heard on the 6 o'clock news every night.
When we got to Sutton we had an Anderson -
actually a Morrison - Shelter in our back
bedroom. I had my mattress on it for about
four years as there wasn't room for a bed
as well.

On 1st December 1941 the Japanese bombed
Pearl Harbour. Outraged, America now
entered the war as our ally. Japan became
our enemy.

One afternoon when the baker called we went
to the van getting bread, when we became
aware there was a dog-fight going on over
our heads. A Spitfire and a German fighter.
On this occasion the German lost and the
plane started to crash and we saw two
parachutes descending and we cheered.
War makes everyone vicious.

In 1941 after Pearl Harbour the USA
came into the war. We were no longer alone.
It wasn't until 1943 that I felt the tide had
turned towards the Allies and I then believed
that we would win.

Fig 11
A Morrison table shelter in the ground floor of a
Grantham house. During the daytime the sturdy
wooden structure was used as a table; at night a
double bed was made up underneath and the
occupants were protected if the house received
bomb damage. Note the candlesticks to provide
an emergency source of lighting.

*"We became
aware of a
dog-fight
going on over
our heads -
a Spitfire and
a German
fighter"*

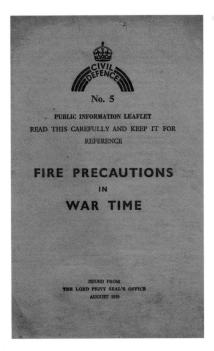

Fig 12
Public Information Leaflets such as this were widely distributed throughout the War – and in the months preceding it. Their purpose was to prepare the civilian population for air raids and possible invasion by the enemy and to reduce casualties and damage to property.

George Smith

"There was a lump of shrapnel as big as my hand"

It was the night previous to the bombing on Kirkby by Bain. We lived in a cottage on the hillside, about two fields from there. There was a lump of shrapnel as big as my hand came across the first field and hit a horse, came across the other one and went through a double brick wall in the washhouse and stuck into the other side of the washhouse. It were a pity that were. Oh yes, and turned over in bed … you could see the moon through all this todo. I was forgetting that one.

It had been a quiet Saturday night. We'd gone to bed, you know I'd got a bit tired. We'd often had to firewatch a couple of nights a week. Aye, it broke Mother's window didn't it?

(Another voice)
You said you was with your horses and they came over that afternoon. They'd dropped those bombs and you said about the Irish just now.

GS
Oh yes, sowing clover seed. The next field that the aeroplane came over and of course I didn't take any notice because I didn't mind, didn't think they'd get any Germans in the middle of the day like. And they started dropping bombs. It was a Wednesday afternoon. Oh yes, some Irish lads was there and they was running and shouting that they was neutral. Down they dropped and they dropped the bomb.

(Another voice)
We all ran for shelter.

GS
You did yes. You was potato picking or setting or something wasn't you?

(Another voice)
Anyway he went over to Alford.

GS
I never knew that. I never did know that.

(Another voice)
He hit a school, a playing field, with some bullets for the children. Anyway they brought him down the other side of Alford that day. What about when they did your [thrashing] drum down the field there?

GS
What the engine? Well it blew a hole in the engine – blew the chimney off. It was one that was parked up as it happened. That was when they dropped the bomb in the pit and your uncle came to the door to see what was the matter. It blew him up the passage – far end – and they cleaned the pit out. They

dropped one right in the middle of the duck pit – a bomb – cleaned the hole out - blew part of the buildings down didn't it?

(Another voice)
That was when you had your land army girls.

GS
It was after that. It was when that building, where uncle lived, it was turned into a land army girls' hostel at Top Park Farm. By the dump, nearly to the top. I know I used to roast potatoes for them every day by the engine shovel, on the fire. They used to come with the potatoes and – roasted. Aye, there was some good gals there.

I remember once coming beyond Mareham on the Hill. It was as black as the ace of spades it was. It was about five o'clock one morning and I was riding up the road and, all of a sudden, it was broad daylight, just like broad daylight. And it was some German bombs coming over and they dropped the Very lights to see where they were. Of course

Fig 13
Land girls at Manor Farm (Baker's farm) Folkingham in the harvest field. Their task would have been to pick up and assemble sheaves of freshly cut barley, wheat or oats in stooks (like the one behind them). Hard-wearing 'bib and brace' dungaree overalls or something similar were worn.

I stopped and got off me bike. Well, you stand and look don't you? And they dropped the bombs at Tumby Woodside. They went over Hameringham and Mareham on the Hill. You couldn't imagine how black it was and then to just break out, because they had some wonderful lights, Very lights what they used to drop.

Very lights were flares fired from a Very pistol either from the ground or from an aircraft.

We couldn't travel at night very well with [traction] engines on account of fire. As soon as you opened the [firehole] door it was just like – light up the sky – you see it was white hot in them days, a terrific light.

Gas masks, they took me to Horncastle drill hall, the soldiers did, because I hadn't a one with me and I was in trouble. They said I'd lost it, government property. And there was this old chap with the whiskers and he was telling me what I should do and what I shouldn't do. I suppose now what I said would be cheek now. That time of day of course they didn't used to bother then what they said…then he finished with me. 'Yes,' he said, 'don't do it any more. Get off home'. I said 'Hold hard a minute. You brought me. You'll tek me back', I said, 'Me bicycle's over at pub.' I said 'I'm not walking from Horncastle, you brought me.' Anyway they took me back home.

One or two years we went sheep clipping, clipping sheep – if you know what that is. I didn't care for it because them bugs used to bite you – sheep fags. I never did care a lot for it at all. Then other times you used to go doing any agricultural work – green spudding…tates like that. But when war were declared – we had one year we did – that was when – can you remember it probably? Well you wouldn't remember – it's daft me

"All of a sudden it was just like broad daylight"

saying that to you. But they came out, the government said they thought they was going to invade so one Saturday all we did was carry out all the implements there was in the yard and put them in different parts of the grass field so's that the aeroplanes couldn't land. 'Cos the field was flat. Used to take horse rake or a wagon or a cart and dump it round about.

And also we had a mock airfield here at Bleasby. Can you remember it? There was – wooden aeroplanes and all sorts plastered out in the big field. There was a make-believe but I don't think it ever worked.

They had some wooden aeroplanes. They had a field here just from Bleasby. We used to go mowing the long grass when it was grass like. They were like decoys. This was out Bleasby way. They stored bombs down Kirkby Lane way, bomb alley. Caistor Street was full from one end to another. Piles of bombs. [Caistor High Street is a road which runs across the Wolds from Caistor to Horncastle.]

'The Dambusters' was the title of a famous film made commemorating the raids over the Ruhr dams in Germany. The Squadron Leader was Guy Gibson who flew from Scampton aerodrome and who became very famous as a result of the success of this raid.

Kit Lawie

But really Mother was such a calm person that she – I think she did it in order to keep an even keel. And also we had to be fairly tactful with German prisoners in the house. I can remember the news coming out of Dachau and all the concentration camps and these men didn't believe it at first but they were brought a film to Moorby War Camp and shown these atrocities and they were devastated. They really didn't believe it. But of course we didn't have the general run of

"He found three airmen in flying gear and boots hiding behind some trees"

German prisoners. We had a batch, come to work on the land, and picked suitable ones out that could live in.

One was a – Peter – he was a carpenter from the Black Forest, a very quiet village man who built a bacon smoker for us and mended all the farm gates 'cos through the war we couldn't repair anything; we couldn't get wood but he utilised all sorts of wood to make gates. And he, strangely enough, was the man that was guarding the Möhne Eder Dams the night of the Dambusters. But, strangely enough, we had him in the house and, who should we have also, was the Dambusters raiders themselves.

The story that I have recorded somewhere about my father, going back to 1943, my father was shepherding sheep one Sunday morning and going to the Home Guard for ten o'clock [he] went down the woodside, and found three airmen in flying gear and boots hiding behind some trees. And he, thinking they were Germans that had crash landed, called them to come on out. And they said 'It's all right – we're English, we're English. Where are we?' But, apparently, on an exercise, before the Dambusters' raids they'd been taken out on a closed lorry from Woodhall Spa aerodrome which was attached to Coningsby and dumped there. They didn't know where they'd been dumped. They'd been driven round for hours and dumped and they'd got to get back to their camp without being caught by the local police or the Home Guard, our Home Guard. So my father said, 'Well come on home…' (because they'd spent the night under a hedge in this plantation) 'Come on home and you can have some breakfast with us', you see. And he brought these three men home.

I remember distinctly them coming up the drive and Father was so fussy – he'd found these three airmen and we were going to feed

Fig 14
Keelby's Home Guard photographed in full
uniform with rifles and other weapons.
All Lincolnshire towns and many sizeable villages
had such a unit comprised mainly of men beyond
the age of active full-time service and mainly in
reserved occupations. Their main duty was to
patrol the local neighbourhood at night-time.

'em – 'cos we'd always got eggs you see and bacon in the house. But when he opened the door my brother was all in his Home Guard uniform ready to go on duty and they thought they'd been trapped you see. They thought this sly old devil had hauled them home in order to capture and have a bit of glory. But Mother said 'No, take no notice. I don't know who you are but come in and I'll cook some breakfast.'

Anyway we were enjoying ourselves helping these three airmen … As they went away they introduced themselves, this would be six weeks before the Dambuster raid perhaps, as Squadron Leader So-and-so and somebody Temple (who they both called Shirley at the time) and he said 'I'm Guy Gibson.' Well the name, strangely enough, didn't mean anything to us at that time you see but they did say as they said goodbye and thank-you and we gave them some scraps of map. We sent them through Claxby Pluckacre hoping they wouldn't be caught because it's a gated road you see and on the Monday morning (this was a Sunday, thick fog), on the Monday

morning – one of them biked back to tell us they were first back and got the award you see. Strangely enough we had the German that guarded the things – but of course six weeks later – Oh, as they went away this Temple, who was the least senior of them, whispered to my brother 'You watch the news in a few weeks' time; we're on a special thing. You'll know when you hear it what it is', and six weeks later they did the Dambusters' raid. As soon as they said Guy Gibson we immediately sprang to it and realised that we'd had them in the house – and it was very exciting really.

Richard Sharpe

Yes, the prisoners of war they were billeted at Ewerby. I remember we had – well this would be later on in the war because we hadn't any prisoners of war at the beginning – Germans and Italians. And I remember the Germans they were all good working chaps. And the Italians I remember they took me father's eggs, hens – well they would take them (back to the camp). They were a bit lazy. If there was any hard work they kept out of it if they could. The Germans and Italians both came from camps in the Ewerby area.

Well it was one Saturday night, I was on my own I think. Suddenly a knock came at the door and I opened it and there was a big fellow with a dagger down his front. Well, I thought … it must have been fairly early on because I thought the Germans had arrived, you see. But anyway what had happened, he'd set off in a – from south west of the country to patrol the Bay of Biscay for U-boats then they came back and they got lost – it got foggy and they couldn't see where the landing strip where the aerodrome was and they came right across country and they were running out of fuel so they decided to bail out over land – I think the man who

"I opened the door and there was a big fellow with a dagger down his front"

Fig 15
Girls from Christ's Hospital Girls High School,
Lincoln, together with two Italian Prisoners of
War and a land girl, picking potatoes at
Mr E Barker's farm, Branston Booths. There were
several camps for Italian and German PoWs in
Lincolnshire and they were regularly employed on
local farms. Some school girls also worked on the
land in holiday periods, especially to help with
the potato harvest in the early autumn.

landed near Anwick he was the first one and
they bailed out all the way across to Boston
and let the plane go in the North Sea. But
I actually went to the field where, it was near
Hardings, Black Fen sort of thing, and I
actually saw where his bottom landed, sort of
thing. Well it was soft landing and he lost one
of his boots on the way down so that there
was one foot with a boot on and the other you
see all his feet.

Well the Hardings, they had a waggoner used
to live there, looked after the horses … Well
he was, he landed about a field or two away
from this and he saw these buildings and he
knocked on the door and then the waggoner
he showed him where Anwick, the village,
was and he walked across and he was
wandering about on the roads and one of our
workmen saw him and, you know, he spoke
… We were one of the few houses that had
got a telephone at that time and so this work-
man he brought him to our house. So I rung

"We were
one of the
few houses
that had got a
telephone at
that time"

up Coningsby I think, Coningsby Aerodrome
and eventually, about midnight, they came
and picked him up.

He just sat, just sat – he wouldn't sit on a
chair or something, he just sat on his knees
on the floor. He was an American.

Joyce Crisp

Well if you want to know one little story –
'cos they used to come across the land – it
was just like a real invasion. They were doing
the hedges down there. Then you'd got to go
and fence 'em up again like – keep cattle in
and whathaveyou.

I think it was probably the government tanks
that came but it was the Home Guard mock
invasions. And they would go through your
fences into the yard or whatever like. They
would leave chaos behind you like.

There was once … you had the Stickford lot
and the Stickney lot and then these others
which was another group from somewhere
else (I never did know where they came
from). And one Sunday morning there was
this mock invasion on and there were, well,
if you want the name it was Ken Rolletts –
unfortunately he's dead now – and he stood at
the top of one of Dad's stacks and he saw the
tanks coming, and the enemy coming if you
like, and when they got to our corner he put
his hands up. He says 'The enemy's here.'
Of course they had to stop the whole caboose
then. But he stood up there with his arms
waving and saying 'The enemy's here if you
want 'em.' But we had the blockhouse like
and, you know, we'd got machine gun
carriers in there, in that blockhouse because
it was a bigger one than a lot of them there.
There were little ones but ours was one of the
big ones.

Afterwards we had to go round mending all
the hedges. I think Dad got compensation for

to do it with like, you know. But we had it to do. Oh, we had a lot of fun, like, considering that it was…how frightened we all were. You made your own fun.

Both Italian and German prisoners of war were brought to Lincolnshire.

The prisoners of war came in the army trucks like. You know they were brought out like. They were in gangs if you like. But yes, they were sort of brought like that and worked the day and then took home in the van. They were good workers. In fact they were very nice people. I mean, like some of them said they didn't choose to be took a prisoner or choose the war. They just had to do as they were told. They were as nice – and a lot of them you could understand just the same as us like. We got, well Jean me elder sister, she got friendly with that but there was one in particular that ('cos we used to go down to help Mr Dracas sometimes when it come to picking tatie time). He was a bit better than us. We only had a plough to do ours and we had less acreage. But it was generally Halliwells that we went on 'cos it was Michael Halliwell's Dad that was there then, and that, but if they went somewhere else that was a bit better off they would have a [potato] spinner, like, that would go round and that and they would have things – and you would get friendly with some of them and one of them made me a bracelet out of some perspex and a ring as well. It was only like, a bit clumsy and that, but it was a ring and it was, you know, a keepsake. The bracelet was like a snake, it was ever so nice, yes. Clear perspex, yes. Oh they were ever so nice. I mean – OK there was nothing to be frightened of. You was probably wary because you'd say 'Oh they're Jerries and they come and bomb us' but no, the prisoners they said they didn't choose the war like. A lot of them

was more against it than – well I was going to say than what we was. Some was for and some was against anyway wasn't there? There always is that. You'd want them to be treated well. The same thing like that but I mean it's their atmosphere – their attitude to us – you couldn't help but like some of them like and that. And they never said or did anything wrong like. They just got on, or they would help you out if you got behind. Yes, 'cos I mean it was all hand work like.

I can't remember the name of the prisoner who made the bracelet. I don't know whether I ever really knew. You know it was – no, I can't remember any names no.

"We had a lot of fun considering how frightened we all were"

Fig 16
A dramatic poster issued by the War Ministry and widely displayed throughout the country. The aim was to encourage people to invest in war bonds and hence make a direct contribution to the war effort.

Dorothy King

Louth was absolutely crammed with servicemen. Airmen and soldiers – everywhere nearly. There were no end of aerodromes around here but they didn't talk about it.

They came into Woolworths, particularly on the toilet counter but they didn't get it like they do now. I should think they get an allowance of toilet things for themselves, soap and things. They bought it all. They used to come into Woolworths you see. No Americans, a lot of Poles, a lot of girls married Poles.

On 5th December 1940 two incendiary bombs were dropped on the malt kiln in Louth which contained hundreds of tons of barley. The fire was too big for local firefighters and nine pumps were sent from Grimsby.

We didn't get anything that you'd call an air raid in Louth. There was the odd bomb dropped. We thought they were going home and they got rid of it. They were being chased probably. We got several odd bombs, they weren't targeted on anything except once when they tried to bomb the railway and they got the malt kiln instead. It burnt and it was full of barley being made into malt and it was useless and we bought a lot cheap for the chickens. Of course the chickens were on rations and this was a bonus. The whole of Louth smelt of burning corn.

The sirens were always going. I don't think it ever went when I was in the shop. It was more the first year or so. I think they were siren happy. We got that we just didn't bother about it.

"Father made the pantry into an air raid shelter"

The Government advised people to set aside a 'refuge room' with specific reinforcement against the effects of blast and splintering. It should be a room with as few doors and windows as possible. In some houses a cellar could be used but in the King household the pantry seemed a suitable place.

Father put some sleepers over the pantry ceiling because the pantry was the most enclosed place. They made that into an air raid shelter. I didn't go in it much, I went once or twice but it was cold and it was miserable waiting in the pantry for the All Clear to go. I absolutely declined to go. Mother went quite a lot but I didn't. They just sat. It was Mother that went [in the shelter] but Father didn't bother to get up after the first – and she got used to it. Nobody was killed that I ever heard of, not from the bombs. They got some windows broken and things like that.

On 30th May 1942 1,047 aircraft under the command of 'Bomber' Harris were sent to bomb Cologne. The target had originally been Hamburg, but three successive days of bad weather made that target unsuitable and Cologne was the substitute target. The total was made of 602 Wellingtons, 131 Halifaxes, 88 Stirlings, 79 Hampdens, 73 Lancasters, 46 Manchesters and 28 Whitleys. 41 aircraft were lost. Nearly 500 civilians of Cologne were killed and thousands made homeless.

Well, there were always Spitfires about. When I was hoeing the garden in the hot summer I used to think I wished I was up there, nice and cool. There were Spitfires always about – guarding the coast because we weren't so far from the coast and at night the bombers went out and I remember one night it was, I think it was past midsummer … and the planes started to come, the Lancasters, and swarms of them came and started to go round and round Louth spire and more and more came until the sky was really nearly black with aeroplanes. Finally they started to go in formation. Now, over the coast … We understood afterwards that it was part of the 1,000 bomber raid when Churchill ordered a saturated bombing of Germany.

The bombing of industrial targets and the civilian population was one of the tactics of World War II. An article published during the war declared: 'These are German bombs – ours are better'. This was not much consolation to the 60,595 civilians killed by enemy action in Britain during the war. Roughly half of the fatalities were in London; comparatively few Lincolnshire civilians were killed by enemy action, but the propaganda obviously induced fear into children.

Hilary had been to the pictures in 1943 as a child of eight and saw a graphic information film about butterfly bombs, warning people not to pick objects up from the ground. A Government poster of 1943 read: 'Beware of these bombs which are very destructive and meant to do you harm.' In fact the only time these bombs fell on Lincolnshire was during a notoriously heavy raid on Grimsby and Cleethorpes on 14th June 1943 when 66 people were killed.

Hilary Healey

And this affected me a great deal. I remember walking back from the bus because the bus stopped at the corner near the Post Office and we had to walk down to the Green where the vicarage is at Nocton and I was holding Mother's hand and there was something lying on the ground, like the lid of a tin can or something, and I was walking right round it to avoid it. I thought everything on the ground was a butterfly bomb and would explode. I was very much affected.

"I thought everything on the ground was a butterfly bomb and would explode"

Fig 17
A poster distributed by the Civil Defence to warn of the dangers of anti-personnel bombs. Butterfly bombs, with their scatter of large quantities of shrapnel, were designed to kill or maim people rather than damage buildings. The real name of the butterfly bombs was Splitterbombe SD2.

CHAPTER 3

WAR CHANGES LIVES

School; evacuees; Land Army; nursing; WAAFs; war-time regulations

From September 1939 the Government organised the evacuation of children from possible danger zones in towns to country areas. Evacuation was voluntary but having evacuees billeted on one was compulsory. Posters declared 'Caring for evacuees is a National Service'.

Joan Parish

During the war I was at the John Spendlove School [at Alford] but it was classed as the Council School then. There was a great shortage of teachers because most of them had gone to the war to fight. The classrooms were very full – 50 or more and our lessons was often disrupted by having to go for gas-mask training down in the trenches at the bottom of the field. We had no sports' day, not much at all in the way of recreation. Went every day on the school bus. The windows in the school were taped up with brown tape in case of the splintering of glass. I can remember we had very good school dinners – rice puddings and stews.

"The school windows were taped with brown tape"

Oh yes, there were lots of evacuees, mainly from Hull and Grimsby. They found it a different life coming to the village. They were used to piped water, water loos and things like that. Whereas we had a pan in a shed and my father used to empty it once a week and this had to do for a loo. They found the food very different because, obviously, they didn't have gardens and my father had a huge garden and this is how we managed to live. He killed a pig, grew our own vegetables. Was quite lucky really as regards food.

One of the National Service options for women was to join the Land Army and some 80,000 young women were despatched across the country to work on farms, filling gaps left by men who had joined the armed forces. The hours were long and the work was often hard. One week's holiday a year was allowed.

Ellen Jackson

Anyway with Mr Holland and two or three big nobs in Coningsby got me to join the Land Army by getting Lady Beryl Groves because she was the one that you had to – that took the enrolment like you see. And that's what it was.

Fig 18
George Applewhite of Heighington with milking pail and stool. Milking was a twice daily task carried out by hand on almost every farm and small holding. During the war milk and dairy products were more readily available to the country dweller than to his counterpart in the town.

And then Mr Gerald Harvey said, 'Well I can do with you, you can come here.' Yes, so I did. He was at the Red House then at Coningsby, the milk dairy. We used to milk cows; wash all the buckets and the coolers and everything right down. Then we'd finish that and we'd go to breakfast and after breakfast we used to go back again to work – and sometimes look out before breakfast, if the cows was in, milk them after breakfast and muck 'em out afterwards. 'Cos that was in stannings – proper stannings [standings]. We used to have the wheelbarrows and muck forks and wheel the – and the muck.

In summer time when it wasn't quite so bad we used to swill it all out with brushes and water and then, before lunch, we used to go down the banks mowing nettles, mending fences or – you know. You worked at the side of a man, there was no kidding about it. You was younger, it didn't matter then. It didn't bother me. My parents were from the farm, you know. They knew what Dad was doing and all the rest of it. I could see that.

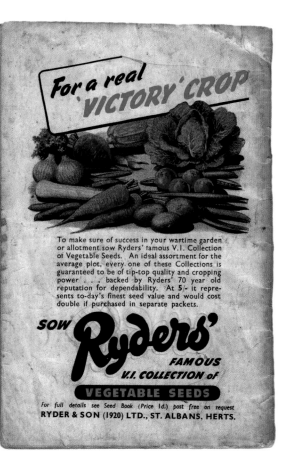

Fig 19
The back cover of the Ministry of Agriculture's booklet on wartime gardening. Firms, such as Ryders' which produced materials or machinery concerned with food production in the wartime, were generally profitable unless they had previously relied heavily on exporting goods.

I was always a bit frightened of horses though, always a bit frightened of horses. Not to mean, I was always – we had three horses on the farm. But then you'd go home for your lunch. Then of course afternoon - started milking again – half past three, you know. You were milking perhaps while six o'clock at night. And you'd all that washing again to do. If the cows was out at grass, in the grass fields, take them out, make sure they was all right, plenty of water, often fill the tubs up and that was your day's work done. Mind you, you were ready for it because you had to be up in the morning half past five, six o'clock.

We didn't go to bed very late. Oh no, my mother would never let me stay out late. I never stayed out far. No I didn't I was really a sort of a – I was a loner, as loners go, but we had some good times, but we had to be in by a certain – by nine o'clock or half past. Then – because it was no good – you couldn't wake up in the morning you couldn't.

In the evening sometimes there was Young Farmers. There was quite a lot of young lads sort of hanging about.

"We had to be in... by nine o'clock or half past"

Spilsby Woman

My brother was an engineer so he joined the Royal Engineers and was put in charge of the first ever bomb disposal unit – a dangerous job. I still have contact with four of the Hagnaby lads and meet two of them regularly at the July reunion at East Kirkby. The decoy was disbanded in 1940 when the East Kirkby aerodrome was established.

During the time at Lincoln County Hospital we were somewhat sheltered from what was really happening outside the hospital largely due to the many posters reminding us that, 'Careless Talk Costs Lives'. Also we were very busy, with little spare time, and earning the huge sum of a shilling a day [5p].

Lincoln was surrounded by aerodromes and there was a modest degree of social life. Occasionally a party of twenty nurses would be invited to a Mess dance and, very infrequently, we were allowed to hold a dance in the Nurses' Home and invite friends. One day the Nurses' Home received a direct hit from a German bomb. One corner of the Home was completely demolished including my bedroom. As I was on leave at the time I had a fortunate escape. No-one was killed but one nurse was injured.

"About five of the armourers died and I was rescued"

Vera

Then I decided that it might be a very good idea, as my friends were joining the Air Force, I suggested that it might be better to go in the Air Force than the army. The family weren't terribly thrilled but I volunteered and I had to go to Lincoln when I joined up. And from there – my first drome, well it wasn't a drome, it was a training session because I wanted to be a driver, an MD driver. So I went to, oh goodness me, I must try and remember, Wales, Porthwelli, and we did a ten-week training session. I could drive

before because Father taught me to drive when I was seventeen. Anyway we did all our square-bashing and I passed all my necessary – oh dear, excuse me I'm eighty so my memory is a bit sort of dotty at the moment, so you must forgive me. It's a long time ago, sixty years.

The war had started when we moved house. We went to live at a place called Little Steeping, near Spilsby. And an old rectory, and it was really rather nice and I wasn't really too bothered about leaving home. Anyway, off I went. And I was in the Air Force and I was stationed – my first drome was Scampton, the Dambusters' Squadron 617, and of course everything was quite exciting – things were beginning to happen then. And I was there for about, oh, six months. Then I was posted to Dutton then from Dutton to Fiskerton, where I nearly drowned. If we wanted to go to Lincoln we had to go on the ferry and this particular night it was very cold, it was in November, and some friends and I caught the … went to the boat. Well it wasn't a terribly wide river but Fiskerton river [Witham] was quite a fast-running river. Anyway when we came home too many people got on the ferry and it turned over so it was rather grim. About five of the armourers died and I was rescued. I hadn't put my greatcoat on, thank goodness, and if I had I probably wouldn't be here today. Anyway that was my first adventure.

Then I was posted to, now where was I posted to? Oh, East Kirkby and from East Kirkby, yes, I was there for about a year or so. Then my mother was taken very ill so after a lot of, sort of, discussions I was allowed to go home on a, oh dear, compassionate posting – to Spilsby, to 7 Squadron and there lots of amazing things happened. We had…our runways were bombed and it was quite a – and two squadrons were shot down one night – and there were about three kites came back out of about two squadrons which wasn't very funny. But life was like that during the Air Force. People don't seem to realise today how really grim it was and how many lovely people we lost.

Anyway, one particular night the armourers had been sent away or given instructions for a new fuse and one of them made a great mistake and turned the fuse in the opposite direction and the bomb dump went up. Unlucky for me, I was driving past the bomb dump and – a mighty blast and, poor old me, I had quite a nasty sort of experience. I was blown off my feet. Anyway, I managed to recover quite quickly and I picked up one or two of the armourers who were staggering towards my garry [military vehicle] and I took them to the hospital. I stayed in the hospital for about four hours helping as much as I could. It was a case of every hand to the pump as it were.

In June 1940 the Government arranged overseas evacuation to the British Dominions. Churchill denounced the haste with which some families rushed to apply as thoroughly unpatriotic. Although most children did reach other shores a German U-boat torpedo sunk one evacuee ship and more than 70 children were killed so the plan was abandoned.

Noreen Farrow

My next door neighbour's nieces, who lived in Grimsby, were sent to Canada by boat. I thought it was very exciting and almost wished I could go – little thinking how long they would be away. In fact one of them stayed and married in Canada and didn't come back to Grimsby. Later a ship was lost carrying evacuees and I lost my enthusiasm for travel. I had a letter from the Employment Exchange asking what I would rather do –

join one of the forces or go to work on the farm. I wanted to work on the farm. I loved working with animals. I love all animals.

Up to working on the farm I was involved with doggies, that's it. After working on the farm, cows, baby cows, one bull (who I didn't like) and a baby bull who wasn't too bad. The first thing I had to learn to do when I went on the farm was to milk a cow by hand.

The first farm I was sent to was only a small farm and there was only, maybe, six cows and that's where I learnt to milk by hand. Didn't stay long there because when I'd sort of got used to milking a cow by hand, after many kicks and upturned buckets, I was sent to this bigger farm where the cows were milked by machine. On the second farm there were more. Oh gosh yes, twenty odd.

They started building a new cow shed shortly after I got there and it was built on the other side of this little stream which meant going over the bridge to get there and, when it was finished, all the cows had to be tested for TB and those that didn't pass couldn't go in the new farm, in the new cowshed. They had to stay in the old one and were finally got rid of so that all the cows in the new shed had been tested and passed the TB test.

The day started at sixish – go in, feed the cows, put the food out, start milking (we had milking machines now). In the summer time, yes. In the winter if it wasn't too bad. In the summer time they were out day and night. There was more than one house. There was the house where the farmer lived and I had a bedroom there. And there was another house where two families lived. The farmer's wife just did the cooking. She fed us. Well she fed us that lived in the farmhouse.

When it was harvest time I used to help with the harvest – not a lot. It was full time work,

"I was blown off my feet"

more or less, looking after the cows and cleaning up after them. I did a bit of hoeing in the field. Hand hoeing, learnt to drive a tractor. The cows were Friesians, black and white – and the bull was a Friesian too. We had a baby bull growing up.

There was one time when one particular cow was going to be shown but I don't know much about it. All I know about it was that I tried to take it down the cowshed with a collar round its neck. It had to learn how to be led. But I didn't lead the cow, the cow led me. Slithered straight down the cowshed. Very messy it was too because the cows had just gone out and when they're on their way out they relieve themselves.

George Smith

Hundreds of 'em – landgirls. They were quite good some of them. Some of course – it wasn't natural for them to work though was it? I mean you take somebody out of a shop or anywhere and you give 'em a man's job, which they did, some went to plough. 'Cos I went with a girl for nearly two years that used to plough. They were quite good really. All the farmers had different ones you see and they went from farm to farm in their own area you see. We see a lot of 'em.

"The horses had been taken away because they ate too much"

You saw a lot of prisoners of war, both Italian and German. There was a camp back by Moorby. There was a camp wasn't there? Prisoner of war camp there. There were Eyties and Germans. Well they came to work you see, along the farm.

We had evacuees from Hull billeted on us. I think it was before the blitzes. I remember seeing when Hull was bombed. I remember seeing a glow – you know…a fire, you know, looking northwards.

Well, a party of evacuees came and my mother – she sort of got her eye on one lad

and she thought he looked a nice lad and so we decided … he was about my age as well, probably a year younger or so. But – anyway, he eventually he didn't like it; he got fed up, and started walking back – to Hull. Well, they caught up with him through Ruskington one way or another. After that I think he went home.

Dorothy King

The family consisted of Father, Mother and I. We sold the shop in Spilsby in October 1938. We were about a year in the [rented] bungalow before we got started you see. We'd plans to pass and all that sort of thing. I think it was the middle of summer 1940 before we eventually got in. We brought a big chicken hut with us and our furniture had been stored in it while we got somewhere to go. Well this chicken house went with us and we bought about a hundred hens.

We bought some from Alvingham in the next village. We hadn't had any in the meantime. They came in crates in a cart with a mule – yes, it was our neighbour. He was a shepherd. The horses had been taken away because they ate too much when the war started – and he worked for Mr Sharpley and he substituted the horse for a mule. The mule kept going all through the war and these hens came from Alvingham and Mr Sharpley had given permission for them to go into the field. Of course they would do the grass good scratching about and they got part-living.

Soon after that we got a smallholder in the village that had a horse and plough to plough up the top half because we got notice that we'd got too much land for a private house and must plough land round the house under the jurisdiction of the WarAg. [War Agricultural Committee] The limit of land you could have without getting involved with the WarAg was an acre I think. We had just

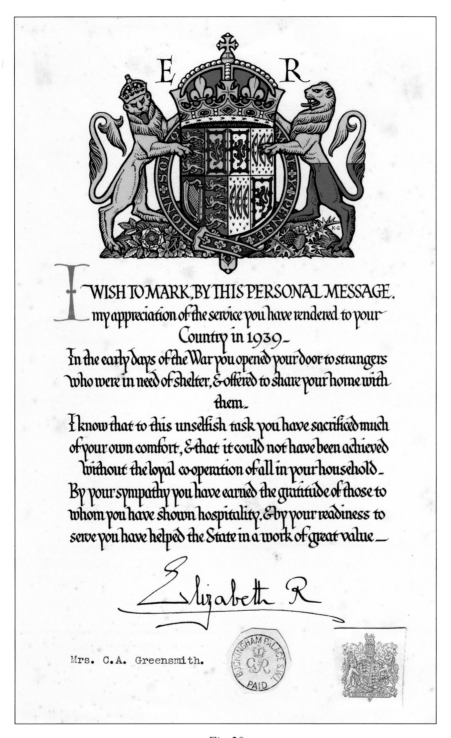

E R

I WISH TO MARK, BY THIS PERSONAL MESSAGE, my appreciation of the service you have rendered to your Country in 1939.

In the early days of the War you opened your door to strangers who were in need of shelter, & offered to share your home with them.

I know that to this unselfish task you have sacrificed much of your own comfort, & that it could not have been achieved without the loyal co-operation of all in your household. By your sympathy you have earned the gratitude of those to whom you have shown hospitality, & by your readiness to serve you have helped the State in a work of great value.

Elizabeth R

Mrs. C.A. Greensmith.

"We had evacuees from Hull billeted on us"

Fig 20
A letter of thanks to a Lincolnshire vicar's wife for accommodating evacuees from Leeds. Thousands of children in large cities considered to be in danger from bombing in the early years of the war were moved to the relative safety of the countryside. Lincolnshire took hundreds of boys and girls from Hull, Sheffield and other regional cities. (The signature on the letter is that of Queen Elizabeth, later The Queen Mother.)

very few yards over the acre. Two men came and measured it.

We planted raspberries and blackcurrants at the very top. Of course we had a vegetable garden of our own and we built a greenhouse and we grew tomatoes. What had been a sort of a home garden we grew chrysanthemums and sweet peas because we'd another neighbour that went to Grimsby with produce every Tuesday and Friday to sell to the stallholders in Freeman Street market and he collected anything that we could grow and took [inaudible] The WarAg? We heard no more of 'em. Our idea had been to keep a couple of geese or something to keep the grass down, we realised we'd far more garden than we wanted but that didn't come off.

In December 1941 the National Service Act was passed calling up all unmarried women between the ages of 20 and 30. Later this was extended to married women who did not have young children. By 1943 90% of single women and 80% of married women were working.

Dorothy King

And then of course I was called up. I can't remember what month it was – to go before a Tribunal. I took a doctor's note because my father was lame and my mother was suffering from the results of two strokes and the doctor said they should not be left at night. So I went before the Tribunal and they decreed that I must do something with food distribution and I would go to the whatdyacall it? It wasn't the Job Centre then and they sent me to Woolworths and Woolworths put me on the toilet counter.

"They sent me to Woolworths - that was my compulsory War Effort"

That was my compulsory war effort. On this counter I worked with a girl whose brother was manager of Larders – and we knew the Larder family – and when their men were

called up they enquired if I could be transferred to them and I went there after about a year.

Stewed Rabbit

Ingredients:

1 rabbit

Sprig of parsley, 1 teaspoonful mixed herbs, 2 cloves (all tied in a piece of muslin)

3 ozs. Bacon fat

1 oz. flour

1 onion

salt and pepper

1½ pints water (about)

Method:

Joint the rabbit neatly, cut the bacon into squares and fry it for a few minutes, then place it in a casserole. Quickly fry the rabbit in the bacon fat and transfer it also to the casserole. Then fry the onion a light brown and place in the casserole. Add the flour to the remaining fat and fry until brown. Then stir in some of the water. Mix until smooth. Add the rest of the water, stir and bring to the boil. Pour the liquid over the rabbit and the onion. Then add the salt, pepper, parsley and herbs. Cook in the oven for 4 hours with the 'Regulo' at mark ¼. Remove the bag of herbs and dish the rabbit neatly with the strained gravy to which a little browning may be added.

From
'The "Radiation" Cookery Book'
19th edition
November 1936

CHAPTER 4

WAR AND DAILY LIFE

Family events, weddings, babies, food

Japan and America entered the war following Japan's attack on Pearl Harbour on 8th December 1941. On the same day Japanese aircraft bombed Singapore and their forces invaded Malaya. Both the United States and Britain declared war on Japan on that date. From that time Japan became allied with Germany until the end of hostilities.

Dot Hurdman

Then Tim came back from Belgium and we got married. Then of course he went out to Egypt for another year and, in that time, we'd planned to have a baby – and we certainly did. He left me pregnant. I had a baby about ten weeks before he was demobbed from Egypt.

We had a honeymoon during that month he came back from Brussels and that was a year and a half after we were married. We had a honeymoon, three days in London which was wonderful, wonderful to go to London. We'd seen everybody off on the train to London time after time again, you know, but we never dared to go while the war was on. However, after VE day we went and had three wonderful days in London – except that it was difficult to get a cup of tea. The Americans had virtually taken over and they drank coffee. All the cafés everywhere were serving coffee. They didn't really consider the English boys. Another thing, while we were on Westminster Bridge, with Big Ben in the background at nine o'clock, I was the only one on the bridge and Tim took my

photograph. And minutes after that Churchill came back – it was the night before the first general election – Churchill came back from his last tour before the election. He was sitting in an open car – you know how the hoods used to come back – and he was sitting on top of that with his microphone and coming along the street escorted by motor cycle. Tim and I were the only ones on the bridge. He gave the V sign and said, 'Good luck to you soldier!' I cried all night. It was really wonderful. We said 'Good luck' to him.

We had our honeymoon a year and a half after we were married and Churchill wished us good luck. It was wonderful!

Vera

The food was beautiful. We were very lucky because Father was shooting all the time. We lived ... well, pheasants and beautiful roast beef and we'd kill two pigs and we had butter from the farm and we had eggs from our hens. But one time during the war, towards the end, one night Father was on the Observer Corps and Mummy and I, I don't know – we felt a bit uncomfortable and Pauline wasn't feeling very wonderful. Mother said, 'I've got a funny feeling something's going to happen tonight.' And it sure did. About an hour later a great explosion was going on the aerodrome because we weren't very far away and so, anyway, we sort of sat it out and a calm descended after a while and Daddy came home and he said, 'Oh dear me, what's been going on?' Then there was some more and Father, he'd sort of scarpered upstairs and

"Churchill gave the V sign and wished us good luck on Westminster Bridge"

underneath the stairs was a cupboard where the cat used to have its kittens. We used to put the apples and that and straw them down and then, after they were all used up the cat used to go in there and have her kittens there – well he said to Mummy after this other explosion 'Elizabeth, take the girls and go under the stairs quickly' and he went upstairs, went in the big gentleman's wardrobe. And he got in the wardrobe and pulled the door to and couldn't get out and we lost him. And we kept calling 'Where are you Dad?' and he said 'Over here'. So we looked all round the house then we realised that he'd shut himself in the wardrobe. It was hilarious really. You know we never really took anything terribly, terribly seriously.

"Then we realised he'd shut himself in the wardrobe"

Edith Taylor

Yes, that's right – married May 6th, 1939, seventeen weeks before the war started – so all our things were new, including household linen, etc. So when the war did start I didn't feel that I was going without anything as we were well set up. But when war started my husband had to go for a medical – which he didn't pass, only grade 3. So in one way I was lucky, he was at home with me all through the war except for a few weeks when he had to go work at Manby aerodrome – and he lodged in Louth. And on Fridays they had to go to a Government office to claim some assistance allowance because they were living away from home and I think it's twenty five shillings a week.

And when he found out, there was rumours at least, that they was going to build an aerodrome at Great Steeping he asked for a transfer. And a man there, a young man there – very power-happy (he didn't know anything about it, it was nothing to do with him). So father says 'Can you make enquiries and see if I can be transferred there so that I can live

Fig 21
The Ministry of Food arranged the production and distribution of National Dried Milk, a good alternative to fresh milk, with the advantage of a relatively long shelf life

at home?' Anyway that went on for a few weeks and one Friday he went in and this man says 'Your transfer's come through to Great Steeping but where it is I don't know.' My husband says 'It doesn't matter you knowing. I know.'

So he came home so he was at home nearly all the time. They did have to go to Kettering – Cyril Goodrig and he – they were going together. They got all the tools and everything ready and it was cancelled at the last minute. So I was lucky to have him at home.

Our eldest child was born 1943 when things were extremely scarce then and my mother had kept the gowns that she made for me when I was a baby and she brought 'em out and the baby wore these gowns for the first three or four months. And then I couldn't feed him myself and there was National Milk then but the nurse I had then said 'Well it's all right I think but they put too much weight on. If you can afford Trufood or Cow and

Gate that's the best. So of course only the best was good enough for our baby so we fed him on Trufood. Then the children were pretty well looked after. We had free cod liver oil and free concentrated orange juice that we used to fetch from the Food Office down Boston Road.

Oh yes the baby was born at home. Nurse Skepporth she came at first but Nurse Courteney – she was my nurse. She came to see me a few months before the baby was born. She said, 'I'm your nurse.' I said 'You're not very old for this work.' She said 'I should think I am. I'm twenty three.' And she was a good girl. She was a good girl – very. Oh yes, I had him at home – in bed nearly a fortnight. Then got up – feeding him on Trufood – but we managed to get nappies. I think the Government did all they could for the next generation you see – this and that. My mother was a one for saving things in case they came in and she had everything that was mine when I was a baby – that's right. And I was a good sewer – well, most women were then – well, some better than others of course. So any bits – I made a nice pram cover or two, all that sort of thing.

Oh yes, I got this pram and me 'usband he did the main part up, cream it was. It was second hand, yes, but the hood and the apron was a bit shabby and Frank Surfleet, he made me a new hood and apron for it – brown to go with this cream. So it looked quite nice. It was his trade, upholstery wasn't it?

'Make do and Mend' was the slogan of a famous poster encouraging people to recycle garments and household linen. Thriftiness, darning and recycling woollen garments by unravelling were familiar skills to most people in the 1930s before the war and this was held up as a virtue to enable the country to keep going.

Edith Taylor

So anyway we managed nicely like that. Then for any hand-knitted garments to pull down and wind up into the skein to knit up again. Yes, we was at a meeting at the beginning of the war, some of us, when someone said 'Oh, we shall have to make do and mend.' Poor Nancy Surfleet said 'I've never done anything else.' And, as I say, it was different times altogether. We all managed and of course we was all in it together helping the war effort.

Sugar and fats were the main things that were scarce. We'd a good garden, my husband was a good gardener, plenty of vegetables and soft fruit and all that. But it's such a job to sweeten the fruit but a tip we found out – if you put a pinch or two of bicarbonate of soda in your stewed fruit – it took some of the acid off it – you didn't need so much sugar. And then one Christmas – of course there wasn't such a thing as ground almonds or anything like that, we used semolina as a base and, I should think a little bit of sugar and what else but that was the main ingredient, semolina. Well it wasn't so good as the real thing but it did work.

And then I'd an old kitchen grate. We couldn't get black lead, but somebody came up with the bright idea of black boot polish for the grate. It didn't work very well. And then, going back to the children, my - handy, you know – making toys. And I made soft toys. I made a golliwog out of a black velvet waistcoat I had before I was married. And my mother sorted some brightly coloured bits left over from dressmaking to dress him and he looked lovely.

[with reference to her husband]
He was working on 'drome down at Steeping. They said, 'Take a packed lunch' and one of the men from down there, from Mablethorpe

"Put a pinch or two of bicarbonate of soda in your stewed fruit"

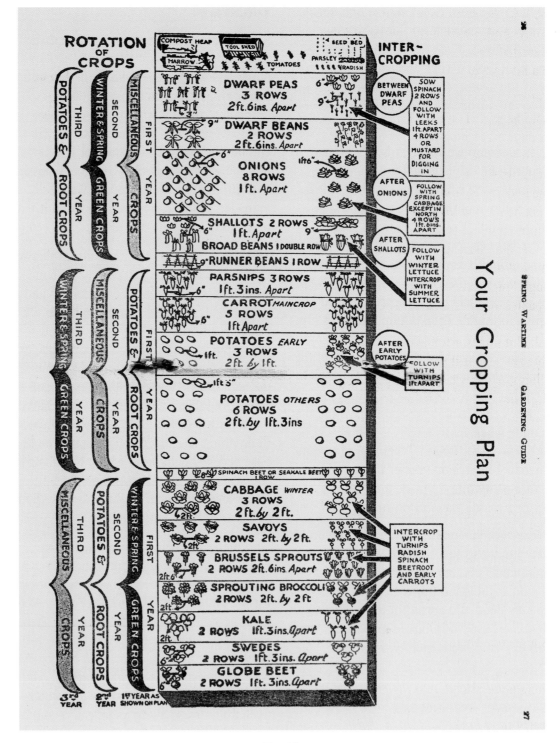

*"We 'ad a
good garden
and me
'usband
was a good
gardener"*

Fig 22

*A detailed allotment planting guide from a wartime gardening book. Much of the produce was
picked in season and eaten fresh; some fruit and vegetables could be stored or preserved for
eating at other times. There were also usually local opportunities for marketing surplus produce.
In some areas products were bartered and money did not change hands.*

so he said, he came with some stuffed chine one day. And Father were telling me about this stuffed chine … 'Oh it's gorgeous, I'd like a bit of that …'

I said 'Do you think he'd sell you a bit?' 'Well,' he said 'I can ask him.' So anyway next day, 'yes' he says, 'he'll bring you some tomorrow when he comes.' And Father was waiting for him coming with this stuffed chine and this fellow had forgotten it and I think he did the same next day. But when he did turn up with it there, sort of, enough for two – small appetites I should think. Well, I enjoyed that. Father said 'I think you've had enough,' picked up what was left and took in the pantry. After tea I kept walking in the pantry picking it with my fingers until I'd finished it – then I was sick all through the night. Yes … but it was a luxury same as lots of things. Meat was … liver and kidney and that, if they 'ad it. I remember going to the butchers to see what they'd got. He said:

'There isn't anything. You've 'ad your ration.'

I said 'a bit of offal or anything?'

'No, I don't think I 'ave.'

'Righto then I better go to see if I can get a bit of fish.'

'Well, I might be able to find you a little bit of liver.'

And that's how we 'ad to manage. But, as I say, we 'ad a good garden and me 'usband was a good gardener so we was all right for that.

Although we was lucky my relatives was farming at Alford. You know…we'd get a rabbit, you get various bits like that – and pig cheer, homemade sausages and suchlike – that was a treat … but otherwise we'd manage and, as I said it before, we was all in it together and we was all helping the war effort.

Joan White

My husband had a very busy time during the war because the mechanics at the dairy were called up and of course lorries had to be repaired. They couldn't be spared for repairs in the daytime so that was a night-time work – and, having worked all day on other work, he had to take in the lorries and repair them overnight for collection in the morning again. Sometimes this had to be done half in the garage, half out, because the garage entrance wasn't very big, you couldn't get the lorry inside so it was half in, half out. It didn't matter what the weather was it had to be done.

The entertainment in the village consisted of whist drives, village dances (in the school of course because we'd no village hall at that time). The whist drives – the desks had to be rearranged in the school; for the dance, which followed the whist drive very often, the men had to haul the desks out into the playground, cover them with the farm stack-sheet and down went the talcum powder on the floor and we danced – sometimes to a trio. There would be a piano and the accordion – oh and drums that we got sometimes. Sometimes it was just the piano which Edgar Davis often played for us didn't he? And he only had one hand with a metal hook or prong on the other one somehow. He did very well with it.

Also we had film shows. We had a 9.5 Pathé projector, so had Mr Middleton, the secretary at the dairy – identical machines. So that night the desks could be stood up high, making a projection platform, and the others arranged for seating in the school and we had Pathé 9.5 films from London. They were quite big reels, I can't remember how long they were. One that was a great popular show was George Formby and that consisted of three or four reels. So one projector loaded up and showed and the other loaded up ready to show. So we did a continuous show in the school.

"Down went the talcum powder on the floor and we danced"

Clothes factories were requisitioned for making uniforms and material was soon in short supply. Clothes rationing actually began on a coupons scheme in mid 1941. Later in the war 'utility' clothing was introduced to standard quality and specified materials agreed by the Government.

"Curtains were made from old bell tent mattress covers"

Joan White

We were married during the war in 1940 of course. Coupons were just beginning to take hold then so it wasn't a white wedding. That was at Willoughby church and, unlike today when we hire premises for the receptions, this was held in my in-laws' house. They cleared out a lot of the furniture from the living room and pushed the other to the side and put up some trestle tables and a meal was prepared in there for the guests.

Fig 23
A pair of knickers, made from English cotton fabric and stamped with the wartime utility mark. This mark was used on manufactured items such as clothing and furniture to give the customer an assurance of quality.

Unfortunately for that day, the best man couldn't come. We didn't know until the night before. He was only stationed at Saxilby but he couldn't get leave. So my nephew was home from the RAF and he became best man. But he hadn't brought his best suit with him. He'd only got his working suit so on the morning of the wedding we had to get – the bridesmaid, my grandmother and the best man-to-be had to go to Louth, Burton's shop, to buy him a suit. Grandma went to see that we behaved ourselves. She wouldn't stop at home and so, in the end, we had a best man and he was well-dressed.

And the day finished – we set off for Chesterfield to take Grandma home and we were going to stay with her for a day or two for the honeymoon and on the [way] we met the man who had been going to be best man on Saxilby Bridge in the pouring rain, waiting with a bottle of wine.

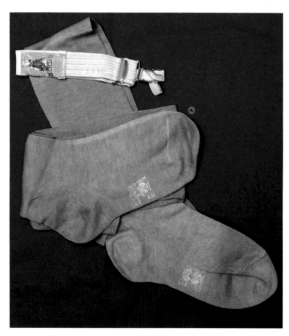

Fig 24
Lisle stockings and suspenders

As for materials for making, I suppose I didn't fare amiss because one of my

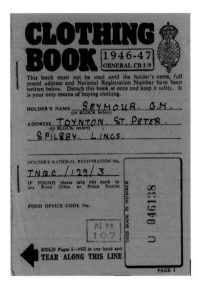

Fig 25
A book of clothing coupons.
Clothing was rationed during the war and
into the 1950s. People became very adept at
re-fashioning old garments and making new items
out of whatever material came to hand, including
on rare occasions parachute silk.

sister-in-laws lived near Lincoln and she got to Newark market, cattle market – they were farmers you see – and apparently, I don't know if it was there (I think there) and, so maybe through the Airforce at Waddington, she managed to get hold of materials for dressmaking. They weren't exceptional quality but they were sufficient. And of course there were rayons in those days, a lot of them, and not very good material. So probably we didn't do so badly.

I know that when we married I wanted some curtains and some of them were made from old bell tent mattress covers, khaki. They also made shirts and they made women's aprons for working. And parachute nylon was another material we could get. That was useful; and flour bag. Flour came in big bags in those days and they would make pillow cases. It's amazing the things we found uses for like that.

Many Lincolnshire villages did not benefit from mains water and sewerage until the war was over. During the latter half of the 1940s and the 1950s huge strides were made in the modernisation of rural houses.

Hilary Healey

Mother did try making butter and cheese with the goats' milk but really butter was too much hard work with hand churning – no mod cons for that. I remember bowls of cream sitting there and skimming off the cream. I loved the goats' milk; it had white cream instead of yellow cream. The cream was always white, it didn't go yellow in the way that cows' milk does. Another exciting thing that happened – again I can't be sure this was actually in the war was that the facilities if you like, a big old kitchen and the water was pumped up from a soft water cistern that was under the big back yard somewhere. Yes, pump water. And we used to take it in turns – there was a big pump – we used to take it in turns to do a few pumps every day – pump into the cistern in the house. And it turned out that the cistern was not all that far from the cess pit. It was before the days of septic tanks and at some point, sister and I were away at school at the time, probably just after the war, the lady who came in to help Mother from Potterhanworth – and she came in one day and found them both collapsed. [Your parents?] Yes. So this was a warning to us all about bugs getting in from one lot of water to another. My father put up a little notice in the bathroom – what had happened. Since we moved there the big old bathroom which was a huge room with a bath in the far corner and the lavatory which was half way up the stairs behind two baize doors and we had a new bath put in and a new toilet put in in another bedroom – because it was a big house with lots of bedrooms and an attic which we didn't even use.

"She came in one day and found them both collapsed"

So he put a little notice over the tap in the bathroom with a verse on it and the verse was:

> Friends, do not for a moment think
> This tapwater is fit to drink.
> Au contraire, it is most inferior,
> And full of very foul bacteria.
> So if you have a raging thirst
> Get well water – but boil it first!

Noreen Farrow

"We ate cooked young nettles, almost like spinach"

Year after year bad news and very few bright spots. We listened to the six o'clock news. As a child I missed bananas and oranges became a very big treat. We picked rosehips and blackcurrants to make syrup because they were rich in vitamin C. We ate cooked young nettles, almost like spinach; ate dandelion leaves to eke out lettuce leaves.

As time went on it was very difficult to get new clothes. I was a very tall girl and grew very quickly. My gym-slip was very big for me when it was bought for me aged eleven. In 1940 we went to Nottingham to see some of my mother's sisters. My mother took advantage to go shopping and bought a blue Harris tweed coat. My father berated her for buying a new coat as this was the day the battleship HMS Hood was sunk. That was Mother's last new coat until years after the war ended.

The Ministry of Food was established in anticipation of war in 1937. Ration books were distributed soon after war broke out and butter, sugar and bacon were rationed nationally from January 1940. The following month meat, fish, jam, biscuits, cereals, cheese, eggs, milk, canned fruit and sweets were added to the list of rationed foods.

Ernie Bogg

We were better off living in the country as we had a big garden where my father grew potatoes and other vegetables for use throughout the year. To get other supplies, our ration books had to be used – so in that way we were limited. I went without sugar in my tea to save it for other things, like baking and making jam, as jam was also on ration. Bacon was rationed to about two slices per week and meat was also on ration. My father had to hand in his bacon rations so we could have a pig, which we fattened. Dad usually killed a pig once a year when it weighed about 30 stone.

Fig 26
Rosehips are rich in vitamin C.
Many country housewives had a recipe for making rose hip syrup.

I don't remember milk being rationed as we were always able to get what we wanted. We also had chickens in the garden so were able to get our own eggs. Eggs were also on ration.

Father would not allow us to have an air-raid shelter as he was buried in a trench during the 1914 -18 War and he was terrified of being buried alive again. He thought them very unsafe, as they were always below ground level and always filled up with water. We therefore went in a cupboard under the stairs with Mam. Dad would go outside and stand in the garden. I was usually too sleepy to remember much about times under the stairs.

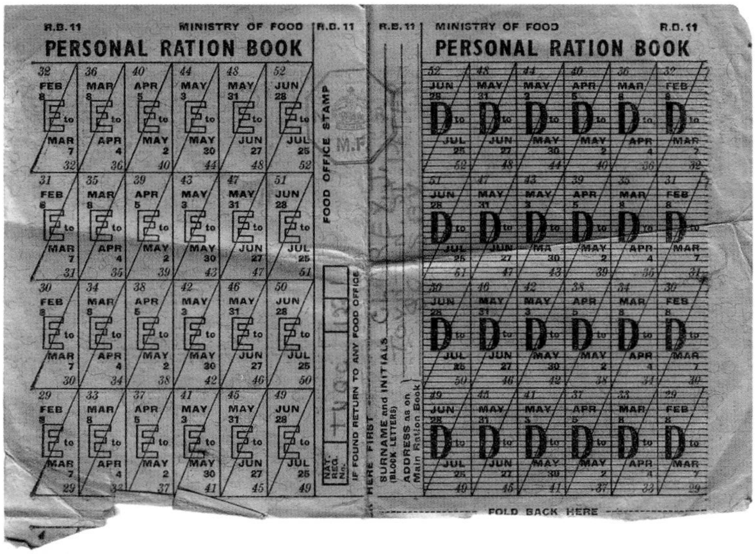

were two parachutes came out. They actually drifted from Bilsby, which is not very far over, onto land at Farlesthorpe where one of the tractor drivers had his gun on the tractor with him and he took 'em in and handed 'em into the police.

Yes, people had to give in metal for the war effort. All metal railings was cut off at ground level, all gates taken off. Some of the gate posts went as well but a lot of the gateposts were left behind – you know the metal ones.

I remember in the wartime they showed us a film, it was a war film, at the cinema in Alford, where your ticket, or the price of your ticket to go in, was a piece of iron or newspapers – anything like that to help the war effort as they called it.

Fig 27
Pages of sweet coupons from a wartime ration book. When a purchase was made the appropriate number of coupons would be cut out by the shopkeeper and later sent on to the local Ministry of Food Office.

There was the farmer's son and another lady who was looking after them just having their dinner and we heard this machine gun fire. And we went outside and there was the three German planes circling. At that time they would probably be over Well and they did a half circle through Alford, over Bilsby, where one of them was shot down. I can still see the plane coming down with a wing that dropped off in mid air.

Yes, the plane itself was spiralling down; the wing just seemed to float down. And there

That was instead of paying. They had the Alford, it was their dustcart at that particular time, was stood outside the picture house and as you came up you gave them what you were bringing. I had two pieces of iron off a bedstead and that was the price of my ticket. I can't remember the name of the film but I think it was one of the first films I'd ever seen like.

"Two pieces of iron off a bedstead ...was the price of my ticket"

Richard Sharpe

"I put my gas mask on when I went to bed"

Well, we were only supposed to use petrol for working, not for pleasure - not supposed to but he always used to have a horse's collar which wanted mending which he used to keep in the boot of his car and he asked one or two pals round Billinghay area, Ed Gilbert was one, and Jack Babbage was another at Walcot, and so that if he got stopped he was going to Robinson's, the saddlers, and taking the horse's collar because there was a strict sergeant, police sergeant, who lived at Billinghay. I've forgotten what his name was. He lived in the sergeant's house there. I remember that it was on the main road wasn't it – the police station.

Yes, he was a strict sergeant. And we were biking home three or four of us were biking home from the pictures in Sleaford, Picturedrome, one Saturday and he came past and he stopped us and I hadn't got a rear light and he ticked me off about that. So we carried on and when I got home there he was playing cards with my father.

Margaret Harrison

The Rectory also billeted airmen. The canon's wife was rather mean though with her rations. Each one was given his own jar of sugar but her son was given a larger share. So the airmen didn't like this so one day they took the son's sugar and replaced it with Epsom salts. Unfortunately, or perhaps fortunately, Esther Bolam noticed the difference.

Everyone from new babies upwards was provided with a gas mask. School children had to carry them to school every day in a box slung over the shoulder.

Friendships were made with those servicemen and often friendships which continued for many years with them and their families.

Canon Bolam used to come into Willoughby School and I expect it was to do with gas mask training but he would come in and say 'black beetles' and we would all disappear under our desks and put on our gas masks. Some people hated wearing them but I enjoyed it so much that I put it on each night when I went to bed. Just for a short time.

Enemy bombs fell on or near the Clover Dairy in Willoughby on the night of July 28th 1942. There was a direct hit on the dairy purification plant. Nearby the Grimsby to London railway line was partly blocked by

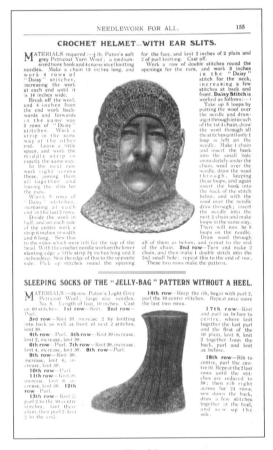

Fig 28
Women (and men) were encouraged to knit warm woollen clothes for men involved in the War. The crochet helmet or balaclava was probably intended for merchant sailors in the Atlantic.

debris. Willoughby church and some residential property was damaged. Telephone lines and railway signal wires were brought down.

I remember the night of the Clover Dairy bombing, for which we didn't receive any warning. Many windows were blown out and especially in the church. I had a lucky escape because they found a large lump of shrapnel had lodged in the ceiling in the joist just over my bed.

My mother often sat up late into the night knitting abwool socks for sailors. Abwool was an oiled wool, water-proofed wool that was used for sailors' socks. The oil in the wool used to affect my mother's eyes and made them go all red and runny.

I have in my possession a small identity card which we was all provided with in the war and it had to be carried and had to be produced on demand – I think it was a police office or an HMS forces man in uniform. Children were provided with these disks and we had to have our name and address and identity number on them. I've got mine, as I said. I suppose it was an identification if we got separated from parents – or worse. The letters for Willoughby were TNPH. My number was TNPH 755 and I always remember it.

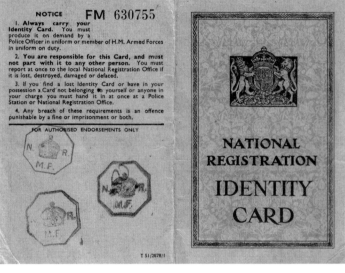

Fig 28
All adults were issued with a National Identity Card which had to be carried at all times and presented on demand to a police officer or member of the armed services. The government introduced this measure to combat infiltration of defence bases and other sensitive areas by spies or other aliens.

My mother was in the WVS and went regularly to serve in the NAAFI at the army camp which was by the side of the railway station in Willoughby. But overall really we were very fortunate I think in the countryside. We had our own pig and we had our garden vegetables and we had fruit. We didn't drink a lot of tea so we swapped our coupons with someone else for sugar and, when my father did work for some of the farmers they paid him in butter and eggs and honey.

And of course we had pigeons and rook pie and we kept caged wild rabbits which were killed off every so often for meat.

My Auntie owned the village shop and when I was six and a half in 1942 we had to write an essay at school about 'The shop I like best'. I wrote about all the things that she had on her shelves – like pop and jam and sauce and then I ended the essay by saying 'but there are other things about which I must not say' – because of course my Auntie kept certain things hidden under the counter which were not allowed to be seen. They were black market goods. My father was always teasing my auntie about her cakes being so dry that they must have been made with dried eggs. Of course they were not because they owned their own hens but

"My Auntie kept certain things hidden under the counter"

Fig 30
Air Raid Precaution wardens in Lincoln.
This was a part-time role; the man on the right,
George Murray, also worked as an engineer at
Robey's. Each wears a greatcoat and 'tin' hat and
carries a case containing a gas mask.

people did have to use dried eggs for cooking in war time.

On my sixth birthday it wasn't possible to buy toys so I had my sister's dolls' pram which had lost its hood and my mother and father made me a doll. The head was made of wood with two glass beads for eyes and sheep's wool for hair. My father painted the head with a rather brownish paint. A curate who called thought it looked like Gandhi. Its body and limbs were made from an old sheet and my mother knitted clothes from pulled-down wool. Old coats were often cut up to make snip rugs and I can remember many evenings when my parents were pulling the snips through the hessian backing to make the rugs.

"The cats kept us supplied with rabbits"

ARP (Air Raid Precautions) wardens and firemen wore a silver badge with the initials ARP topped by a crown. They were civilians called into service from 1939 onwards.

My father was an air-raid warden and we had a metal plaque on the front wall of our house indicating that this was an air-raid warden post. My father was put in charge of the village paper dump near the blacksmith's shop. There was a risk of fire from incendiary bombs when they were dropped and he had to defend this paper dump with a bucket of water and a hand-operated stirrup pump which was pretty useless I imagine.

Villagers were given a target to be met to help the war effort. For Willoughby it was £2,000 in 1943 which was a large sum of money I suppose then. Varying ways were found to raise money for the war effort and to support Forces' Comforts' Fund.

Dorothy King

We always killed a pig, sometimes two. They were always, I should think, about 23 or 24 stone in weight so that was quite a lot of meat. And we'd eggs and tomatoes and vegetables. We none of us took sugar in tea or coffee so we always saved sugar to make jam. We weren't short of meat – but a bit of butcher's meat if we had any visitors we made a stew of beef and carrots and onions and those sort of things. Mother and I used to have the vegetables in the stew and visitors used to have the meat. I don't remember ever getting any fish. They used to come round with it but that stopped.

We got rabbits and pigeons. The cats kept us supplied with rabbits in the spring and early summer; they didn't get them when they were full grown. They used to wander the fields, we'd two cats and you hear them – they were so triumphant when they got a rabbit.

There was a yowl as they brought it home. I used to skin it and cook the lights and the head for the cats. Rabbit pie and rabbit stew and rabbit boiled. You could buy pigeons. Plenty to eat. We'd eggs and the odd hen that didn't look very well – Father wrung its neck.

We made jam as far as we could with the sugar. We bought Kilner jars and you could bottle a lot of tomatoes, they didn't need

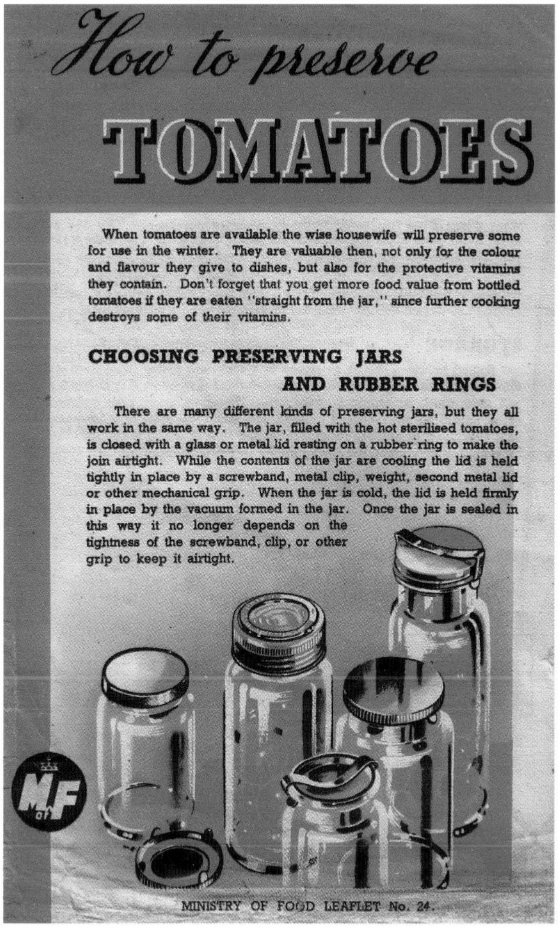

How to preserve TOMATOES

When tomatoes are available the wise housewife will preserve some for use in the winter. They are valuable then, not only for the colour and flavour they give to dishes, but also for the protective vitamins they contain. Don't forget that you get more food value from bottled tomatoes if they are eaten "straight from the jar," since further cooking destroys some of their vitamins.

CHOOSING PRESERVING JARS AND RUBBER RINGS

There are many different kinds of preserving jars, but they all work in the same way. The jar, filled with the hot sterilised tomatoes, is closed with a glass or metal lid resting on a rubber ring to make the join airtight. While the contents of the jar are cooling the lid is held tightly in place by a screwband, metal clip, weight, second metal lid or other mechanical grip. When the jar is cold, the lid is held firmly in place by the vacuum formed in the jar. Once the jar is sealed in this way it no longer depends on the tightness of the screwband, clip, or other grip to keep it airtight.

MINISTRY OF FOOD LEAFLET No. 24.

Fig 31
A leaflet published by the Ministry of Food giving basic advice about preserving tomatoes, a garden product that would be in good supply for only a relatively short period of the year. Most family larders and pantries had rows of sealed jars and bottles with preserved fruit and vegetables. Some food was preserved by drying or salting.

sugar you see – of course they were useful for frying with bacon. We had rows and rows of Kilner jars full of tomatoes – and any fruit that we got. We had to save any sugar.

No electricity at that time in Keddington but we did have gas. We thought we were very lucky, the only person in the village. The gas people were willing to come just over the border. We made black curtains and had sticky tape on the windows, heavy curtains at the door, the front door and the back door. We had to sidle through it – not open the door far; put the light out.

We'd not much money to buy anything with and we'd enough clothes to last us. I don't remember buying anything; we knitted jumpers, knitted a dress. It didn't seem any trouble to get the wool. It was a long-sleeved blue dress. It didn't wash very well. I don't think I wore it a lot – because I didn't go out any. I wore Wellingtons in the garden and I had a pair of breeches, two pairs of breeches that I had at college and I wore those for gardening and they were corduroy. I wore them through the war and after - tough ones and socks.

In the early part of the war we knitted for troops but not after I went to Larder's. [Larder's was a well-known grocer's shop in Louth.] The early part of the war Mrs Staniland, who lived at the big house, she organised glove knitting and chided us if we didn't get a pair knitted a day. She said she could knit two. But then she had a cook and a housemaid – as Mother pointed out to her. Well, it was thickish khaki wool and she said she could knit two pairs a day. Well Mother could knit one and I could knit one if we really stuck to it.

"She organised glove knitting and chided us if we didn't get a pair knitted a day"

A man who could supply game – a grocer and game dealer. He owned Cadwell Park. His full name was Mansfield Wilkinson – he was

*"I was
too busy to
worry and
think about
a possible
invasion"*

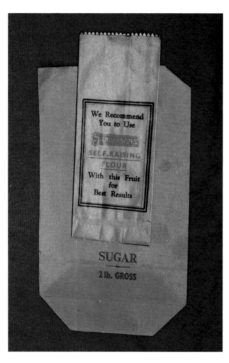

Fig 32
*During wartime and for several years afterwards
sugar was weighed out by the grocer and sold in
two-pound (0.9Kg) bags made of thick blue paper.
Similarly dried fruit (and many other products)
were stored in bulk by the grocer and only
weighed out and packaged at the counter
in front of the customer.*

always called Manty, a short, stout little man
and a large family who all worked for him
and a wife - she worked as well and he would
buy practically anything, anything edible,
either fish, game, vegetables, anything. If you
had a bit of anything to spare in the garden
you'd take it to Manty and he'd give you a
few coppers. A lot of poorish folk did – you
know, they'd get a bit out of the garden –
'a bit of something for Manty'. It all went up
to London 'cos he wasn't far from the station
and all his family and his henchmen packed
and took it … it was quite a little industry …
nothing went to waste at Manty's.

I don't remember really being bothered about
a possible invasion. Too busy to be bothered

… that was my trouble – I was too busy to
worry and think a lot about … there was too
much personal … there was too much to
think about.

I was looking after both parents and
gardening – and working, and going out to
work. You see early morning Tuesday and
Friday when we had the flowers to pick - they
want to be picked fresh you see. I got up at
half past four because he came about half past
seven and they had to be picked and bunched.
Mother used to get up about five o'clock and
she could do that. She could sit at the table
and bunch.

He showed us how to bunch them for the
market and then, you see, there was the pigs
to feed and chickens to feed, the watering to
be done – anything – perpetual hoeing in the
summer and the chickens to see to out in that
field. And they wouldn't come in because it
was double summertime all the wartime you
see and they wouldn't come in to go to roost
until eleven at any rate. If it was a fine night
it would be later. And you couldn't leave
them out in the field because there were foxes
about. It was a very short night on Monday
night and Thursday night. You were so
absorbed by what must be done.

CHAPTER 5

WAR BRINGS NEW DUTIES

Trains; planes; firewatching; King's visit; farming; ARP; Home Guard

Bob Riddington

Being a railway enthusiast I was very taken when a whole lot of army arrived at Willoughby – a trainload of vans – with all living vans for the soldiers to live in; Officers' Mess and Cookhouse and a huge twelve inch Howitzer gun called Achilles. The whole outfit was towed by two ex-Great Western Dean Good engines and they were numbered WD 197 and 198 and I was very fascinated with these.

What the purpose of all it was I wasn't old enough to understand but I was very taken with all these chaps and all these engines and the gun. They once fired it at Willoughby; they fired a shell out to sea, broke all the windows nearly in the village and the station and I always remember they used to have a mobile film unit come to the village school every Monday night.

And I was very pally with one of the drivers. He was a lance-corporal called Tom and he once said to me 'Would you like to come to the film show on Monday night?' So I said 'Oh, I'd love to.' And of course I wasn't all that old. And he said 'Well you come with me. Be there at seven o'clock.' And I went. I can always remember the film was Bob Hope in a film called The Cat and the Canary. It frightened the life out of me and all night long I saw doors and windows opening and I hardly ever slept a wink. Anyway, that was that.

While all this army was stationed at Willoughby of course we had a local factory called the Milk Dairy factory beside the main railway line and one night, when being a local fire – plane spotter, I used to have a paper called Aeroplane Spotter, and I was very interested in all the planes and the bombers and the fighters and, one night, I heard this plane coming down the railway line. I jumped out of bed, looked out the window, and when it followed the main railway line, went past, I thought it was a Bristol Blenheim. Anyway it turned round somewhere near Alford and came back down the railway line. And it was a moonlight night and I suddenly saw there was a cross and a swastika on it and of course it was a Dornier 217. It came back again and then went about as far as Alford and turned round and came back and then there was a whistle and at this whistling, and of course I didn't realise what it was, until he dropped – he let two bombs go and they landed on the main filter beds – blew the filter beds all to pieces; covered the railway line with bricks (a terrible smell) and it broke the windows in the house and it frightened us all. Well that was that.

And I can always remember we had to go at 10 o'clock at night down the village in a little field in the middle of the village. And there was a big old wooden hut on four metal wheels and it was used as a lambing hut for one of the local farmers. It was equipped with a little sort of stove and me and Tom used go at 10 o'clock, I think it was once a week I think it was, (I was still at the Grammar School) and we used to go at 10 o'clock at night and stay till six o'clock in the morning.

"I suddenly saw there was a cross and a swastika on it"

Well one night, I can always remember he used to take a book with him the old chap did. It was always Martin Chuzzlewit, one of Dickens's books, and we used go and sit there and we used to light the fire and sit there and wait for anything that was to happen – if there was any raids or any fires.

Well not long before we'd been sat there, Tom would sit there, he'd drop his book and he'd snore and go fast asleep. Well one night the air-raid siren sounded at Alford. We could hear it and we looked out the window and we could see searchlights and, after about an hour, all of a sudden, this shed moved – rocked backwards and forwards. It woke the old chap up. He said 'Bob, they're 'ere.' He said 'Bob get the bucket – get the stirrup pump and your tin 'at on,' and we got well equipped and the place shook backwards and forwards once again.

Neither of us dare open the door to see what was happening. Finally we plucked up courage, we did, to open the door of this shed to look out and we couldn't see anything. Well, we could see searchlights in the distance all over Grimsby or somewhere and we found out that the rocking was caused by an old cow in the field that was rubbing its backside up agen the shed. Now that was absolutely true and we went back in the shed, Tom went back to sleep and then at six o'clock in the morning, we went back home.

Clarice Driffill

We had tin helmets and we didn't have anything else. One of the men said 'I'll show you how to do it' and he started to run and he ran straight through it ever so quickly. He says 'Now follow me.' Well, we had to get in a line and do this and I saw the others running through before me. I weren't that eager I'll tell you. Anyway I ran through and I couldn't believe it. I couldn't believe that

"The King was due to come through. We were all sworn to secrecy"

I wasn't burned. And he said…no, it's no good stopping in the middle was it? So, however, he said 'That's what you'll have to do to rescue people if they drop incendiaries you see.'

Dot Hurdman

The other important thing that happened was the King was due to come through. We were all sworn to secrecy – it was very, very, hush-hush. The police were on duty for the station. We cleared everything from the platform. We swept the platform, ridiculous really. We arranged ourselves on both sides of the line and waited for the train to come along with the King in it. Thursday night it came at great speed actually. We stood waiting for it. Lydia put her cigarette out. There we were, in our best, and there it was – gone! There was nothing to see. You couldn't see into it, carriages or anything. It just came and it was gone. All the trouble we'd gone to! You can imagine what the comments were like afterwards from the porters.

Clarice Rutter

Making one's own form of entertainment in the long winter months brought out talents regrettably lacking in the new modern ways of life. Friends gathered around the piano for a sing-song following a feast of home-made cakes, ham and chicken rolls, etc. Brass candlesticks either side of the piano music stand gave extra light to the paraffin lamp in the room, and the glow of the log fire added warmth and atmosphere to the friendly setting.

The attractive three storey farmhouse, set amidst horse-chestnut trees, was the home I lived in and loved so much for the early part of my life. Living on a farm in the country, to little children, war seemed far away. The wooden shutters and thick blackout curtains added warmth to the large old farmhouse, much appreciated in winter.

Dolly Wheatley

The shelters were under the railway line, the main railway line that went, I should say it went to Grimsby that one does. Yes, they were under there. There was one or two top ones too, overground ones you could walk straight into, but the others – you had steps to go down into them and we had one that was very bad. The rain used to go in; we had to have duckboards in that one. And if we'd had heavy rain – the ground seemed to be a bit on the slope that went down in – so the rain went in. So we had to get buckets and shovels and bucket it out the next day.

That would take some time, let me tell you. And you'd only got one electric light to work with in the shelter you see but it had to be done. Then we used to dry it up, put the duckboards outside till they'd dried then put 'em back again. Oh, I enjoyed being there, it was good company. Of course there [were] two of the men working there under Kerry but I was the first woman he put on, and I thoroughly enjoyed it.

Before I finished up, oh, we was – well the ARP work pulled in a lot of the decontamination as well. We had that to see to you see – anybody get gassed or anything – and then, if it come a wet day – we would mebbe go into that place and we'd stock-take of all the clothing. There was shelves of it you see, if anybody got gassed they had to go through the decontam and change all their clothing and anything like that. And if we couldn't work outside, if it was a wet day, we'd go in and take check of that you see and make note of it.

Well, I used to do a bit of shopping in the dinner time. And then I got as I used to give me order in at the Co-op on Monks Road and he would see that I got it. Oh, yes it was delivered. And I remember going up to the little shop top of street one dinner time and Mr Hardy came outside to get some vegetables. 'Oh,' he says - Wednesday, they shut at one o'clock then Wednesdays – he says 'you better come in Mrs Wheatley and get served. You've got to go back to work never mind about this lot.' Oh, yes, I was priority. I was right at the end of the queue. But he was very good like that. It would be awkward. You couldn't shop Wednesdays then; you couldn't shop Sundays.

It wasn't far to go. We'd got quite a few shops at the top. We'd got the Post Office, and we'd a bakers up the top. They didn't do much though that time, it was only three days a week, wasn't it? When the Quickfalls had it.

Henry Wheatley

I used to go and fetch the meat on Saturdays didn't I – and queue for biscuits at Dickinson's? I used to go to Dickinson's in Mint Street on a Saturday at eight o'clock queuing for opening at nine. Then I used to go down Harold Gray's to get the meat.

In January 1943 seventeen houses in Thomas Street, Lincoln, were destroyed by a bomb. The Wheatleys, who lived close by, took in one family which had been made homeless.

Dolly Wheatley

Oh yes, we managed quite well but the problem was having the other three in the family you see. I used to cook a meal at night time you see. I wasn't bothered about the children because they had a good meal at school but there was my husband and myself so I used to cook a meal at night. Of course the children shared in – made the rations go as far as they possibly could. And he says – and these three – they had their midday meal. She'd get that but she'd share in with mine at night. I said to my husband 'I can't do it.

"If anybody got gassed they had to go through the decontam"

The rations won't go run to it.' Then, of course, we was killing pigs you see. We heard such a bang one night. 'Oh,' I says 'that's the string gone off the bacon on the landing.' Anyway I went to pick it up and the flies had been in it. So I says to Henry 'You'll have to go to the Food Office' because we wasn't allowed to register for one I think, for my husband for bacon. We couldn't register with the Food Office for him. And I says 'Bacon's gone bad. You'll have to go to the Food Office' which was this end of Silver Street, and I says 'Just put a complaint in for it.' I'd no problem – we got it straight away so we got that sorted out.

We'd got our own chickens and we had the garden stuff you see so really we didn't do bad. We had our own vegetables and our eggs and the bacon you could say but, we really didn't do bad. Then there was a dairy on the bottom, just on Winn Street, just past the Abbey and I could take a jug that'd hold two and a half pints of milk and I could take that to her and she'd fill it for tuppence [two old pennies]. That was skimmed milk but it made nice milk puddings and custards you see so I was all right that way. And the family they all took sugar. And I said to them 'It's no good. You can't have sugar in cakes and puddings and in your tea and in your coffee.' I said 'you've got to go without.' So they went without in their teas. And they still do. We still go without. Me 'usband he couldn't go without but what bit he took – it wasn't much…but you couldn't rely on anyone else giving you any coupons.

"So they went without sugar in their teas"

But the main thing was well of course all clothing went on what we called dockets. One of my neighbours she was buying curtaining for her girls to have dresses made of – it wasn't on coupons you see, curtains wasn't. And sweets and everything you got a monthly ration and, towards Christmas, I used to put it

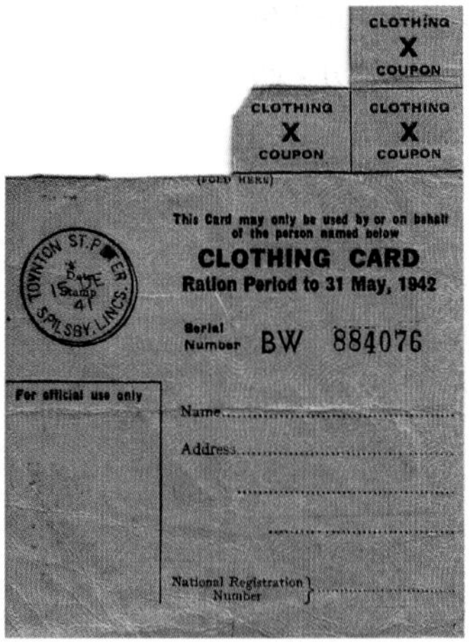

Fig 33
Part of a clothing card with coupons.
The card was initially issued to the customer at the local Post Office. Unlike coupons for food items, clothes coupons were not dated and could be accumulated to buy an expensive item.

all away. They knew where it was but they never touched it so they all had a good share out at Christmas time with the sweets, yes.

I went to the shop once, to Mr Hardy's - oh no, he'd sold out then Mr Luke'd got it. And a woman came in one Saturday night (I stood at the back of the shop) and she wanted some sweets so Mr Luke said 'I'm sorry. You've used all your coupons up. You can't have none till Monday.' She was a stranger to him – she was to me an' all. Anyway, he looked up; she argued and argued. 'Well,' he says, 'I'm sorry, you can't have it.' Anyway he says to me afterwards 'What was all this about?' I said 'She works at the Food Office. She'd have gone and reported you, you see.' 'Thank goodness for that,' he says.

Lincoln's worst air raid was in January 1943 when a solitary Dornier 217 aircraft flew low over Lincoln dropping incendiary and phosphorus bombs. Four civilians were killed and 30 were injured. In Thomas Street a bomb fell in the middle of the road but failed to explode immediately. The bomb was surrounded by sand bags and nearby houses were evacuated. It exploded two days later and seventeen houses were destroyed.

Henry Wheatley

That bomb dropped on Thomas Street was the unexploded bomb wasn't it? That night I'd finished feeding the pigs up and I said to Uncle Frank: 'Are you ready to go yet?' And he said: 'I've just got the bottom pigs to do.' I said 'I'll wait for you then.' And as we were walking down from one set of sties to the other a plane come over and dropped the flare. It was a German plane, he dropped the flare like. He says 'Get down. Get down.' So we got down onto some allotments then when he'd fed the pigs we walked down onto the allotments which is now the top of Hillside Estate and we could hear shrapnel falling like. And we got between two garages and the shrapnel dropped on the other side of the garage so it dropped away from us.

Then when we looked over the hill, where the Co-op was on Monks Road we could see the fires burning in the town like. They were aiming down the industrial – yes – they were all in the line there with the river – Claytons' Forge and Clayton DeWandre and Rustons, all in a line by the river. They were a little bit off target, oh, it was…And then two nights after that we went round with Bob Leggitt and Dad, didn't we? We went down to John Street, climbed over the wall, 'cos Bob Leggitt had got a lot of papers in his house that he wanted like, in case it got blown up. And we climbed over the wall we went in the house, number 19, and we looked out the window at the bomb, in the street like, and he collected all his papers and what he wanted and we nipped back out again. Nobody knew we'd been in.

"We looked out the window at the bomb"

Fig 34
Seventeen houses were wrecked when a delayed-action bomb exploded in Thomas Street, Lincoln, on the night of 15 January 1943. Several other bombs fell in Lincoln that night, the worst raid of the war for the city.

Fig 35
A bomb disposal team with the unexploded bomb recovered from St Benedict Square, Lincoln, following the raid on 15 January 1943. Quite a high proportion of bombs landing in towns and countryside failed to explode but they had to be defused and made safe – a tricky and highly dangerous occupation for the bomb disposal teams.

George Smith

We might have had a few air raids, the nearest as I can say, to do any damage…I remember once doing firewatch and the neighbour and I was out in the field and it was dark and then they'd been dropping incendiaries more than bombs actually. We heard something rushing in the air, and naturally you dropped flat on the ground, and it was off a container from the fire bombs like. 'Cos they came in like a Molotov basket. And it used to open out and there used to be dozens of them come out. And this was the basket that was coming down. It was rushing through the air. Sounds a bit queer. I still 'ave the piece, the hook, that was up on the plane, I unscrewed it. I still 'ave it to this day.

That's as far as bombing. Early morning you used to see some, hear some coming over.

"It dropped three bombs in the field next where we was working"

And if they dropped any of the Very lights, well it used to light things up for us. You didn't take a lot of notice of that when you was on your own on a bike like in country.

Apart from a bomb on Kirkby on Bain, it wasn't too bad just around the village here. We got some away that didn't affect us much. I was up at Belchford once, grassing there. It was in the afternoon. We looked up and there was a bomber coming of course. We didn't see it coming over, didn't realise I dunno. And it was German and it dropped three bombs in the field next where we was working and there wasn't one went off. As for damage, we didn't see a lot of it. Well the prisoners used to cheer when they saw any that they'd knocked down, and they used to come through on their wagons to work.

(Another voice)

Tell Mary about the aeroplane that came down across the fields.

GS

The one that came down back of Spikings. Well that was the 95 watch. It was Hampden. We see it coming on fire. That was the next door neighbour and I, we was on fire watch. And it came down, and I shall always give him credit, and I know…he was going straight for the village and he was coming down all the time and suddenly he turned like that, the side of the village into a field and crashed there. And he killed all of them 'cos we went to 'em, we got one out but we couldn't - the fire stopped you from…You couldn't do anything.

I always say that he saw the village and he turned that plane and took it away. Oh, there was several planes down round about…There was one came down into the taxi driver's Dad's field.

(Another voice)

George Stone's?

GS

Yes. His Mam and Dad came down (they was a bit mad at the time actually). His father went into a field that had some turnips on it and one of them jumped out and he went up to his knees in the ground. The other got out, went down the road, but he couldn't – he died. Mrs Stone said…And then there was another one came down into them cottages, three or four cottages all in one at the end of…in Haltham, back down through there. Who lived there? Billy Parish's and all them.

There was one came Fairfield, straight for it, and it stopped just before it got to it. They was fairly lucky over that one. It's a job remembering it all. It's so long since.

Kit Lawie

The rules came in more or less straight away. The racing pigeons were commandeered. They either caught them and killed them, thinking there would be a shortage of meat I suppose and all spies of course – well we weren't to tell anybody the way to anywhere because the signposts had been removed and we weren't to help them. As children we thought they were all spies and careless talk about anything at all was frowned on.

I remember the War Agricultural Committee being formed and they went round all the farmers. And these were half a dozen farmers who'd been chosen, presumably for their good farming methods, and they threatened anyone with eviction who were not producing enough food or letting the thistles grow and so on.

Then rationing came in, but we lived at the farm at East Keal on Marden Hill and always had our eggs and bacon and rabbits. I think we were allowed to kill two pigs a year so, in order to get the maximum meat we reared them to be nearly 40 stone before we killed them and therefore we had these flitches [sides] of bacon hung on the wall four inches deep in fat but at least they lasted and they went with the lean rabbits for us to eat.

We never locked our doors, never, and we had no occasion to. There was nothing to steal except really the flitches on the wall. I can't ever remember anything ever being stolen except a bicycle from our back yard when the men at the Air Force camp were late after taking some girl home and they would call and pick up a bike and bike back to East Kirkby to get in at whatever time was their time due in. When we reported it to the policeman he said: 'Oh, don't worry – it'll be in a dyke at East Kirkby. We'll find it.' And they always did.

"The racing pigeons were commandeered"

I mean, domestically, I wasn't the woman of the house, I was the girl of fifteen, sixteen, working on the farm. But I used to go to Boston and queue for things – scarce things. I remember queuing for an hour and a half for one candle or a box of matches – but not both. We could have which we thought. But we, being non-smokers, went for the candle. How we lit the fire is another matter. I think we lit it with a spill from the fire. I once queued for two hours at Day's, Cash Street in Boston for an enamel pie dish that nobody seemed to want, it was the only bit of hardware in the shop. But when I got it home it wouldn't go in the oven so I knew why I could have that then.

"I remember queueing an hour and a half for one candle"

In May 1940 War Minister Anthony Eden broadcast an appeal urging civilian men to become Local Defence Volunteers. These men were subsequently renamed the Home Guard ('Dad's Army'). The public was asked to hand in their shotguns and pistols for use by the Home Guard. Over 20,000 weapons were collected.

The Home Guard was formed of course and they were on Marden Hill minding the high ground because the view over the fen across to the coast was clear. We are on the last hill of the wolds, the southern wolds, and we could see across to the coastline. My brothers weren't in the Home Guard then but my

Fig 36
The Heighington Home Guard unit with their equipment.
In the early days of the war uniforms, arms and equipment for 'Dad's Army' were difficult to obtain.
Many units had to improvise or rely on old or inappropriate equipment.

father was. He was very lame but he was allowed to go into the Home Guard because he'd got the only 12 bore shotgun in the village and so he was very popular. But he wouldn't let the younger members of the Home Guard be in charge of it but my two sons, when they were on duty, they took turns with this shotgun.

The boys, my brothers, biked down to Ingoldmells and Sutton on Sea and patrolled along a length of the coast on bicycles. At least they were meant to patrol on bicycles but they were always punctured and they were mostly pushing them. What they were going to do if they saw a German landing craft I don't know because they weren't in any contact with anybody either telephone or otherwise so I suppose they were going to run.

Our neighbours were also in the Home Guard. They were two brothers but they were a little bit slow at turning up at Home Guard parades so they were arrested, I suppose you'd say, one Sunday morning for not turning up and were given a fine of £4 each which was then equal to about a fortnight's wages really. But anyway, soon after that they realised that they'd have to give more time to getting hay and harvest in.

Ernie Bogg

Well, yes, they said they were volunteers but you'd no choice. You had to go into them – a little bit like Dad's Army actually that you see on telly – it was the business men who were the officers. I think Colonel Jay who was the head of the brewery in Alford, I think he was a colonel in the First World War, and he was in charge of what they called the Alford Division. I'm not sure but I think in the winter time they had to go on manoeuvres and various places – you know for training sort of thing.

Fig 37
These large concrete blocks (with dimensions varying between 3 and 5 feet) were designed to impede the advance of enemy tanks and other vehicles. They were usually placed at strategic points near the coast where invasion forces might be expected to land.

"My brothers ... patrolled along a length of the coast on bicycles"

Richard Sharpe

Another thing I remember – we had to grow as much food as we could didn't we? Because at that time we didn't grow enough wheat in this country, or corn to satisfy everybody. And it used to come across from America, from prairies and all that sort of thing, Canada with U-boats. They couldn't get across while they got convoys then they got while…they made us…well, anyway, every field, every bit of land was ploughed. Yes, and also, down Anwick Fen, fields and fields were ploughed up and what they did was ploughed up bog oak. Have you heard of bog oak? It was all leaning one way as though, in the past history, icebergs or wind or something had blown them all in the same direction. It was dotted about. They were only short bits – the main trunk.

There were several fields you see. No, once you got it out the way it was easy. Also, early in the war when we thought the Germans were coming, somebody thought they'd be landing down Anwick Fen, fairly flat, we had posts stuck all round. You know every twenty yards. It was to stop a plane coming down, or

"He'd got the only shotgun in the village and so he was very popular"

a glider. No, we haven't mentioned farming as such have we? It was gradually changing even during the war.

Because power was originally steam power wasn't it? Ward [and] Dales, you've heard of Ward [and] Dales haven't you? Ward [and] Dales. *[Ward and Dales of Sleaford were steam ploughing contractors, and at one time were the largest such contractors in the country, with 24 sets of tackle – two engines, plough, cultivator, living van and water cart.]* One of my first jobs was carting water to the engines for Ward and Dales. They did steam ploughing. They used to be one side of the field and then the other. They'd gradually move up [the field] you see…The plough used to pass on a cable and they were still using that during the war but it was dying out and they were bringing tractors in from America.

"Father still used horses during the war"

This was during the war because I remember I was so excited when we got our first, when we were allowed, our first crawler tractor. We got it through Fenton Townsends and I biked – you know, met it coming from Sleaford. Well this it.

That's the old crawler – that's an International 2D6. That's a Minneapolis Moline combine and the tank, the corn went up into the tank, and then they had to – the sacks were down here and then they filled the sacks and they were allowed to slide onto the floor and we had to pick them up again because they were too heavy to do with the sticks. We had to have a winding bale.

That's wheat, yes. This was just after the war. Yes, yes, there was a shortage of food after the war. You had to grow all you could. Father still used horses during the war.

Fig 38
The North Road Ironworks of Fenton & Townsend, agricultural engineers of Sleaford. Like other Lincolnshire dealers they sold both home-produced tractors (principally Fordsons) and those imported under the Lend-Lease scheme from USA and Canada, a trade controlled by the War Agricultural Committees. Tractors made up for the loss of horses and farm labourers to the War.

There were at least eight I remember in the stables. The wagoner he had the choice of his first horse and the second wagoner he had the choice of the next.

Oh, there'd be about eight men at least. There was the wagoner, assistant wagoner, we had three yards with the black hole down Anwick Fen, [inaudible] Yard where another gathman worked, another yard at the home yard at Anwick where another man worked so that would be five.

Joyce Crisp

Oh, I would feed all the calves, staying up all night to keep watch when they were calving and pigging - whatever. And when you got up in the morning you fed the things before you went to school. You came home at dinner time if there was some calves wanted feeding or something like that because we got an hour off for dinner at school and then went back again. Then you came home at night, got your own tea if you did first and went out and did the yard work again, feed the things up like again and got your own tea if you'd any chance. 'Cos Dad was out with the horses in the field as much as possible you see. So he didn't have a lot of time for doing the yard work, that was up to us. Then of course we had to milk the cows, feed the calves with the milk from it and the pigs and everything.

We grew a bit of everything as much as possible. Wheat, barley, oats. They was the main things on our farm but other people had one or two different ones. Then sugar beet so that it went on a winter crop for to take up. 'Cos you had to do them so your corn was in the summer time 'cos you couldn't get too much all at once. 'Cos you'd got to, how should I say, your corn in the summer time then came your taties, picking crop, and then your beet. And if you'd had too much you'd got behind hand. So you had to space it out

reasonably well. But you had to do crops that you could sell like the taties you had what you wanted out of it but sold the rest, you know – to get cash. The beet you did and, as I say, you got pulp back and that would feed the animals with afterwards. The corn you stacked it in the yard and you got the corn and ground it up for the meal and that to feed the things with and the straw for the bedding.

It was all converted round and round. You sold it, you got it, you used it. It went round in circles and sold what you could for to get your money. 'Cos that's all you had for living with – no wages.

Well, with us being at home we had to help a lot. This is why - how I come to know how to do the leading of the sheaves and the stouking and all that sort of thing. So I can do all them sort of things like 'cos we had to do. But when it came to threshing – well, you'd got to have eleven or twelve people at once because one had to feed the drum off the stack; and the other had to cut the bands that'd been put round. Everything's got to be done at the same time so one person couldn't go from one job to the other. So then each farmer used to come, where the threshing machine set was going next and where it came from and that, they all used to follow it round, like a gang.

No, we weren't short of labour, not when it came to thrashing and big jobs like that – not that you needed more than one but you managed as much as you could on the smaller jobs or leading jobs. Oh yes. There was the horses. We had to have those.

It was like tractors is today, but it was horses. We only had two horses but I mean that's all we'd enough people to use it with like. You often had to have two horses together for to do a job. But one would often do a job like. But no – horses, cows, sheep, pigs, chickens,

"So I can do all them sort of things like 'cos we had to"

Fig 39
Horses ready to pull a reaper at Frithville. The use of horses in farmwork declined significantly during the war and the majority of farms had a tractor by the time the war was over.

"It was something all the time just continuing round and round"

geese – you name it I think – I don't think we had any goats. I don't remember having those. That's about the only one we didn't have like. But OK that was the horses for to do the land work because that was all you had at the time. Then again, the cows for milking and all that sort of thing and rearing the calves and for to sell the calves to get a bit of money and whathaveyou – and selling the pigs – chickens then came the eggs, and the turkeys and that at Christmas. It was self-contained. That was how you had to work it so that it was something all the time just continuing round and round.

Rabbit Pie

Ingredients:
1 large rabbit
½ lb ham or bacon or pickled pork
Salt and pepper
1 teaspoon of chopped parsley
Grated lemon rind to flavour
(but not during the war)
½ lb rough puff pastry

Method:
Cut the rabbit into joints and the ham into slices. Arrange alternate layers of rabbit and ham with the salt, pepper, parsley and lemon rind in a dish. Add 2 tablespoons of water; cover with rough puff pastry, and make a hole in the centre. Bake for 2½ hours with the 'Regulo' at mark 4. When cooked, pour into the pie ¼ pint good seasoned stock. If the pie is to be served cold, a little gelatine may be dissolved in the stock.

From:
'The "Radiation" Cookery Book'
19th edition
November 1936

CHAPTER 6

WAR AND THE GOOD TIMES

Happy days; companionship; make-up; end of the War

Vera

Well my best memories really was the companionship and the lovely people. And it was also very sad because I was driving and I used to take the boys to the aircraft when they took off and it was awful because up towards the end they were sort of, they were so tired and they were very sort of – they got upset very easily because they'd probably been on leave and their wives were having babies and…I was lucky really because, living at home, Father was wonderful, he used to do me flasks of coffee and put a wee drop of something nice to give them when they came back. And we had these big flasks and I used to put them in the driver's seat in the carrier and when the boys came back, which was always grim because if you were on night – and we were mostly on night duty; they were mostly on night raids. I used to hate it because it was terribly frightening because some of the aircraft lights were shot away and all you'd see was the props whirring and you had to get out of the way pretty quick.

We used fifteen hundredweight trucks and we had to wait until they got in for dispersal. The first thing they did was to nip out and have a sweet pea behind the – they used to rush out behind the other side of the…'Won't be long Tommy' they used to say. They used to come to the window 'Anything good for us tonight?' And Mother would make egg sandwiches and bacon sandwiches, because we killed two pigs, and, bless their hearts, they were really - they were so grateful.

And they used to come and play tennis. Father put up a thing in the mess and said that if they wanted to come and play tennis they could - as long as they sent somebody to mark it out, mark the court out, they could. And my parents were wonderful to them – they really were.

Well, fashion - really and truly we were in our uniform all the time apart from the time when I was allowed to come home for compassionate posting because it was so nice. I could pop into civvies and we had tennis courts so we could play tennis. And – oh, it was…so different to what it is today because

Fig 40
A hand-bag, in imitation crocodile skin, with a range of wartime beauty products: scarf (behind the bag); handkerchief (in the bag); powder compact, vanishing cream, lipstick and toilet soap (in front).

"They used to come to the window 'Anything good for us tonight?'"

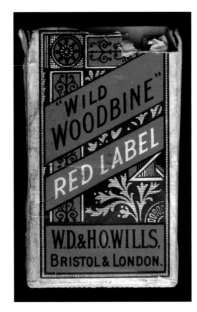

Fig 41
A packet of five Woodbine cigarettes,
which would have cost only a few pence. A high
proportion of the population, both young and old,
smoked either cigarettes or pipes.

there weren't all the amazing things to do –
and the dances were quite different and
people were quite different. Promiscuity was
not rife like it is at the moment. They're
always under the impression that, because we
were quite young, we were having a larky
time but we didn't. It wasn't like that, it was
– we were all – well not in my experience.

*"And we
all smoked
Woodbines"*

Oh yes, we had our make-up. Oh, goodness
me, Cyclax and Elizabeth Arden and we all
smoked Woodbines because we didn't get an
awful lot of money. Father gave me, he
always sent me money each month but you
had to be very careful because we didn't get a
lot of money. So we all used to buy
Woodbines or Balkan Sobranis went down
very well – the black ones with the gold tips.

Some girls drew lines on their legs to make
it look as if they were wearing stockings.
I didn't but a lot of them did because you
spent your life more or less in uniform.

But when we were at home we just sort of
wore the country clothes. Wherever Mother
and Father went together as a family – like
my daughter does, like Anna and Stephen do
now – they do everything together and they
love it. And we did the same. But we didn't
wear the sort of clothes where you, sort of,
painted your legs. In fact I think we wore
stockings. I can't really remember. I think
I wore jodhpurs like the girls do most of the
time – or trousers.

George Smith

You forget you know. Forget who I'm talking
to. I remember a lot of things I daren't tell
you. It's a long time ago you know. How long
ago is it now since it finished? Sixty some
years isn't it? It was '45 when it finished
wasn t it?

It's a long time since. I've had many scrapes
since then. I went and said, 'I will,' for one
thing.

Kit Lawie

But I think there was a lot of humour in the
war as well as the serious things in the war.
The War Agricultural Committee (all right
they watched the farmers) but Whitehall also

Fig 42
Cigarette lighter made from Perspex

Fig 43
Despite rationing some young ladies managed to obtain, or make,
non-utility garments.

sent out a lot of edicts advising farmers what to do and how to go on. It was evident that they hadn't got anyone advising them that knew anything about farming at all.
I remember a leaflet coming advising us how to make a proper midden and my mother, who did all the farm clerical work and everything and she had a very dry sense of humour, she wrote back and invited them to come and view our muck heap for themselves – because a midden is the old word for a manure heap and we couldn't believe we'd been advised how to build a muck heap.

But there were lots of humorous times and, it's sad to say, but life was never dull. There was always something – dramas or something – and our postman, a reliable man, Mr Taylor – I think he lived down Reynard Street at the time. I can't think of his Christian name, he would ride up on his bicycle and he would be informing us as he arrived 'Avenue house burned down last night; there was a landmine on The Gables Hospital' – and he would talk

all the time he was delivering but never stop in his track and keep walking. He would be away again – he wasn't a gossip but …of course we'd no paper. We'd just our radio with the, what we called the wet batteries. They were these charged acid-filled batteries that I used to bike to Spilsby to Rippons to pick up and so that's really how we got our news but even so there were some great dramas going on.

Clarice Rutter

Gymkhanas for charities were held often. On one occasion the Red Cross and St John Sports' committee of the Duke of Gloucester [gymkhana] was held once in Carter's Park, Holbeach. My mother won first prize driving her Welsh pony, Silver Lady, in a governess cart – the pony's mane plaited with red, white and blue pompoms (Mother had made these in wool). The Duchess of Gloucester presented Mother with a lovely driver's whip which I still have.

"We couldn't believe we'd been advised how to build a muck heap"

Mother always did her shopping with this pony turnout; we also rode the pony in our holidays. A road tax licence was charged for use of a pony and cart on the road.

Carter's Park had been given to the people of Holbeach by a very generous man; he also built new cottages for rent. If the tenants paid a little extra rent they would eventually own their own house.

Rationing continued for some time after the war ended, long queues outside the bread and cakes shop. Even small gardens were used to provide vegetables for the family. Dig for Victory poster signs were seen in many places. Young married couples were allowed permits to start their homes, many buying second-hand furniture from auction rooms – or were given items from family and friends.

After the war prefabricated homes were provided for the married couples in Holbeach as the men came home from the war. The wireless ran on accumulators. Programmes like ITMA and Tommy Handley cheered families up during the war time (although mainly saved for hearing news of the war) – and when war was finally over everyone was relieved, with street parties being celebrated. So life could safely continue. Unfortunately many lives would never be the same again.

Margaret Harrison

I remember one time having a photograph taken to send out to my brother in South Africa to show him how my sister and myself had grown and so we were standing alongside my parents so that he could tell what heights we were.

"We were so fortunate to be living out in the countryside"

Overall, wartime memories were very happy memories – times of just happy family times. I think that was really because we were so fortunate to be living out in the countryside.

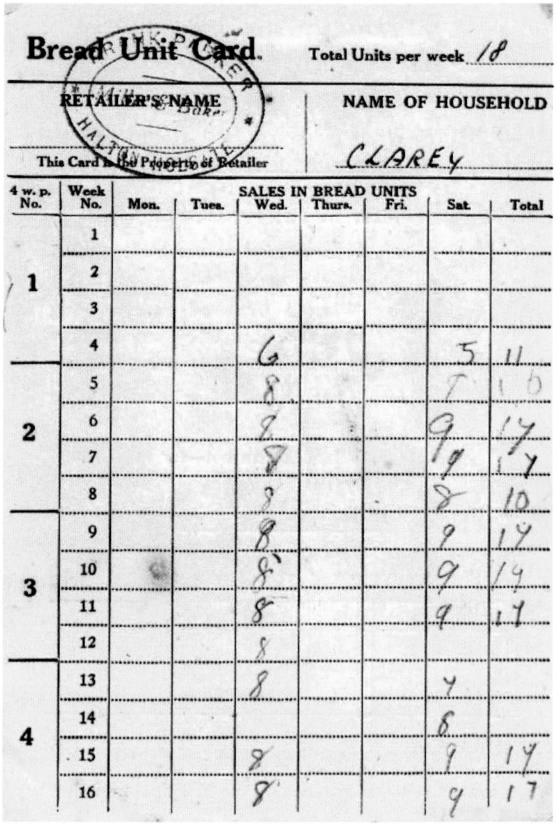
Bread Unit Card. Total Units per week 18

RETAILER'S NAME — NAME OF HOUSEHOLD: CLAREY

This Card is the Property of Retailer

4 w. p. No.	Week No.	Mon.	Tues.	Wed.	Thurs.	Fri.	Sat.	Total
1	1							
	2							
	3							
	4			6			5	11
2	5			8			7	10
	6			8			9	17
	7			8			9	17
	8			8			8	10
3	9			8			9	17
	10			8			9	17
	11			8			9	17
	12			8				
4	13			8			7	
	14						8	
	15			8			9	17
	16			8			9	17

Fig 44
Bread Unit card issued at Halton Holegate after the war. This household of three adults had a weekly ration of 18 units, equivalent to two large loaves.

Hilary Healey

At Christmas time one or two years I remember they used to put out a big tea chest in the hospital there [Nocton] and ask them [Americans] to throw in donations for the village children.

Well, everything went in – razor blades and razors and things not suitable for children – and in particular there were sweets! Hershy chocolate bars and things called Lifesavers. I remember very well they were in a tube like a Polo – they had a round hole in the middle like a lifebelt about the same size as a Polo and they were a boiled sweet and you got different colours in one tube and when these were brought to Father, because he was in charge of some of the handing out. And I remember going round with him to some of the old ladies in the village taking little presents including these Lifesavers and also – I don't suppose we took the old ladies chewing gum, Wrigleys chewing gum which was something we hadn't come across before – spearmint. That was really quite exciting.

Clarice Driffill

[reference to the bomb dropped on Waddington church]

But wasn't it amazing that it should land like that and not do any damage. I mean it was amazing that it didn't kill anyone. It seemed as if….

Interviewer

One person died as a result of that – a Miss Hall. She was hit by a beam in the rectory and died as a result and died of her injuries eventually. But considering there were two huge landmines on parachutes right in the centre of the village with all the population around…

Clarice Driffill

Yes, it was marvellous when you stop to look back. You see, like the summer before that happened, when they was evacuated from Dunkirk and they said no-one had ever known the sea like a millpond before and I remember Mother saying 'It's the hand of God; it's the hand of God.' She said, 'God saved those lads.' And the same with Waddington it happening. She said - Mother used to say things like that and, as you look back, the amazing things that did happen – I know a lot of dreadful things happened but a lot of amazing things happened that you did see…

I mean after you'd been through a lot of what they had all been through sometimes you would think you couldn't help but talk about it, but we got whereby we didn't mention it. You know it was something had to happen and that was the end of that. You never spoke about it and there was people we knew, young men, I could reel 'em all off from school days had all been killed but when you first heard it you sort of felt inside a kind of, I can't explain the feeling now, oh dear, it was awful. But funnily enough you got whereby you didn't mourn. It was happening so much that you were lucky if you didn't – you know you would take it for granted – there was the sadness but there was something, a comradeship during the war what I've never, ever experienced since. I mean everyone was nice to everyone and everyone would help everyone. If somebody had a trouble, or anything happened that someone had a funeral, everyone rallied round. Nobody – I can't ever remember all through the war anyone saying anything nasty.

That's right, everyone was in the same boat and you'd be in a queue – you'd go up town and you'd have to queue for everything, you'd be in a queue and then somebody would say 'Oh flippin' heck, this is getting weary, come on,' and she'd start singing 'Roll out the Barrel' – then all the queue would start singing and it was a comradeship that I've never known since and never before and I don't think I shall ever, will happen, again. That was something nice. You know in all of it there was something that made you feel happy inside. And at work we had the Relay in and we were all, we were allowed to hear the news every time it came on and, if we wanted Workers' Playtime and things, oh they was easy-going, but the thing was we was very busy and you can't be doing office work and typing and listening to Workers…

"But funnily enough you got whereby you didn't mourn"

We used to listen to the news because everyone was so eager wondering what was happening.

The end of World War II with Germany was officially declared at one minute past midnight on May 8, 1945. This was called VE day.

On August 6, 1945 the first atomic bomb was dropped on Hiroshima, Japan, which caused widespread devastation. Three days later the second atomic bomb was dropped on Nagasaki. On August 14 Japan surrendered unconditionally to the allies. On September 2, 1945 victory over Japan was celebrated. This was called VJ day.

Fig 45
The entrance to the Regal Cinema, High Street, Lincoln, with flags and bunting to celebrate VE Day. VE Day (Victory in Europe Day) was celebrated on 8 May 1945 and most communities, both large and small, across the country put up decorations and arranged special events.
(The Regal Cinema, just south of the Stonebow, was demolished in the late 1960s to make way for Littlewoods' store, now Primark.)

Stewed Pigeons

Ingredients:

4 pigeons

½ pint gravy

2 oz. butter

½ lb tomatoes

1 small onion

1 dessertspoonful of seasoned flour

Method:

Truss the pigeons as for roasting, coat with the seasoned flour, and brown quickly in the heated fat; also fry the sliced onion. Put into a casserole with the tomatoes, peeled but left whole. Pour over ½ pint of well seasoned gravy. Cover the casserole with a lid and cook for 1½ hrs.

From:
'The 'Radiation' Cookery Book'
19th edition
November 1936

"It was a comradeship that I've never known since and never before and I don't think I shall ... ever again"

INDEX

*Page numbers in **bold** type refer to illustrations*